HIGH IRON

A BOOK OF TRAINS

"RIDERS SHAKING THE HEART WITH THE HOOFS THAT WILL NOT CEASE"

Thundering up the grade into the Cajon Pass between San Bernardino and Victorville, California, on the eastbound run, the Atchison, Topeka and Santa Fe's crack luxury limited, The Chief, is shown double-headed behind a Mountain-type locomotive (4-8-2) and a Northern (4-8-4). In leash behind the two mail-cars are eight airflow-design, steel Pullmans replete with every *de luxe* detail that has made The Chief implicit with the romantic appeal of modern railroading.

HIGH IRON

A BOOK OF TRAINS

by

LUCIUS BEEBE

BONANZA BOOKS • NEW YORK

HIGH IRON: The main-line or high-speed tracks

Railroad Photograph.

CONTENTS

Lucius Beebe

ILLUSTRATIONS

Lucius Beet

INTRODUCTION

THE most heroic of American legends is the chronicle of railroading. It is heroic not only in the integral sagas whose synthesis constitutes the body of any legend, but in the spaciousness and breadth of its entire pattern, its concern for the affairs of men on a scale essentially epic and its inescapable association with a national destiny.

What her armadas and merchant fleets, her ships and admirals of the ocean-sea have been to England, what the legions and proconsuls ruling the *orbis terrarum,* the known world, were to Rome, steam locomotion and the great railroad builders have been to America. For a full century, railroads and railroading have dominated the story of the nation and they have left a stirring, a breathlessly vivid impress upon the American consciousness. The chapters have been written by the Collis Huntingtons and the Jack Casements, the W. W. Fairbankses and William Masons, the generations of engine-drivers who have wheeled their Taunton-built diamond-stackers, their latter-day Mikados and Mallets over the illimitable steel of the illimitable and compelling western land, and the whole of it is possessed of an urgency and a magnificence that is, in the essential meaning of the word, unique. For no other machine has ever exercised a fascination for the human imagining comparable to that of the steam locomotive.

In the introduction to one of the collected volumes of his poems, John Masefield tells of the sailing ships that peopled his youth standing into the distant roadsteads of the world, "beautiful unspeakably."

The writer has stood in the late afternoon at the end of a bay in the long train-shed of the St. Louis terminal watching the coming and going of many trains. There were locomotives from nearly a score of roads on the tracks surrounding that Pharos of all switching towers that divides the hemispheres of the East and West: the ponderous but fleet passenger greyhounds of the Missouri Pacific, after whose first 4-6-2 type the Pacific locomotive was named, one of the celebrated tribe of the

3

Pennsylvania's K-4s, panting from a scorching run across the whole of Indiana and Illinois under a July sun, the immaculate heavy Pacifics of the Alton, their boiler shells the fine blue-gray of daily polishing, rods and cross-heads and tires gleaming like mirrors, the lovingly tended power of the Frisco with burnished brass bells and hand-rails in the old manner, blue and gold and rakish, backing in for the through varnish for Oklahoma and the great Southwest. And there were the locomotives and the rolling-stock of the Burlington and the Wabash, the Illinois Central, the Nickel Plate, the Southern and the Mobile and Ohio. He has paused by night in the yards at Cleveland where the feline Hudsons of the New York Central panted in the hot darkness, mousing for green lights among the switch points, and the yard engines throbbed with a subdued tensity waiting for the Century, in three sections, to thunder through like the implications of destiny itself. He has rolled as smoothly as on a bath of oil and almost with the speed of thought into the Colorado uplands aboard a Burlington streamliner, and he has sensed the conquest of a continent as the Overland has borne him, in the tranquil security of his drawing-room, within a few miles of Promontory where once Engine 119 and the Jupiter, "pilots touching, head to head," enacted the closing scene of an epic of empire. The symphony of the twelve driving-wheels, obedient to the main rods, of a Union Pacific Challenger-type gliding implacably westward in the yards at Omaha with a mile of red-ball freight behind them has moved him as some men are moved by the "Eroica" or the opening verses of the *Song of Roland*. And the sight of The Chief, double-headed and with a pusher, breasting the high iron of the Glorieta Pass, has been what Masefield's ships were to him, "beautiful unspeakably."

This book makes no pretentions of being a history of railroading in America nor in any sense a rounded version of the saga. Simply it attempts to gather together a number of photographs that have some value for their historical associations or some gratuitous esthetic appeal for railroad amateurs and enthusiasts, and to append thereto a chronicle of some of the trains, locomotives and aspects of railroad history, from the forties to the present time, that have stirred the imagination of the author or pleased his fancy.

William Rose Benét once wrote a delightful poem beginning:

> Green aisles of Pullmans soothe me like trees
> Woven in old tapestries...

and to many and many an American the long green cars, the compact state-rooms, those secret mansions and microcosms of all luxury, the flowers and crisp linen of the diner, the burnished brass of the observation platform, the ghostly whistle of the locomotive far up ahead in the enveloping night and the flickering markers of the passing limited receding down the iron are implicit with all that spells wonder and romance and delight.

The impulses and loyalties of the true amateur of the legend of railroading are limitless and varied, but for most the saga of the trains in some way defines an urge toward the ineffable delight of going places and expresses it in terms of compelling mechanical factuality. Mostly the railroad *aficionado* does not limit his loyalties either to the wistful obsolescence of antiquities nor yet to the magnificence of crack limiteds or the achievements of rebuilt Hudsons with 80-inch disk wheels which give them a cruising speed of 100 miles an hour. He has been known to lavish his enthusiasm on the 700 miles of narrow gage once a part of the Denver and Rio Grande, before it became the D. & R.G.W., and he has stood radiant before some Baldwin Consolidation, loved long since but lost awhile and rediscovered on a forgotten spur in darkest New Jersey. Confronted in the disused roundhouse of some now mighty road with an authentic William Mason, Taunton-built eight-wheeler which had served the line in its first pioneering youth, he is overcome as an antiquarian before a veritable walnut, long-case, month-striking clock from the master hands of Thomas Tompion, or as a connoisseur confronted with a magnum of Château Lafite, '64, recorked and perfect from the ministrations of many faithful wine butlers long dead. To each these are the good things, the delights of earth.

The end of the fifth decade of last century as an editorial point of commencement has been arbitrarily selected because the forties witnessed the justification of what had before been at best uncoördinated ventures in transportation and because about this time there were evolved the form and substance of locomotives and trains whose vestigial traces are still visible to-day. By the end of the 1840's, trains and their mechanical components, their dispatching, control and the administration of railroads would have been clearly recognizable to a reader of this book.

To be sure, as far back as the middle thirties the Boston and Worcester Railroad celebrated the completion of its iron by running Fourth of July excursions between its two terminals and carrying more than 1,500 passengers on four specials, or nearly 400 fares to a train. Many crack trains of to-day have capacities for fewer than 150. The familiar type of enclosed corridor-car with two four-wheel trucks at either end had already been introduced by the Baltimore and Ohio to replace carriage-coaches slung from cantilever springs, and the traffic manager had caused a Bible to be placed in each of the new cars for the persuasion, doubtless, of the timid pious. Operating rules, including provisions for the setting-out of flagmen behind trains making stops between stations, daily comparison of conductors' watches with official time and the maintenance of time-table speeds had been drawn up by the Utica and Schenectady, and schedules differentiating between local and express service and recording the seniority of passenger over freight trains had been made effective on several roads. The thirties saw the beginnings, the forties the youth and the fifties the first fine flowering. And while this book is not historical and aims at no chronological scheme, its concern is not for the infancy of American railroading but for its romantic youth and magnificent maturity.

There has never since been and never again will be a time of such inherent, characteristic romance in railroading as in the fifties and sixties. It was the period when engineers owned outright the great storm lanterns that served as headlamps for their locomotives, embellishing them with antlers and having their side panels engrossed with portraits, silhouettes and pastoral landscapes. It was the period of the eight-wheeler, the American-type locomotive, with its diamond stack, its four high drivers, its brilliant lacquerwork and such balance of design that the makers signed their product as an artist writes his *fecit* forever on a canvas. It is legendary that in winter, when the sound carried clearly, the engine bells ringing across the hillsides of New England were so beautiful of tone as to be loved like the church bells and so familiar that the country folk in villages many miles from the line would say "There is the General Putnam" or "The Minerva is behind her time to-day." The conductors were known as "Captain," and, in cold weather, the brakeman carried the key to the cannon-ball stove in every car against fares who might be prodigally inclined with the chopped wood. The roads had about them the romantic promise of great things to come and the friendliness which until recently existed on country trolley routes, where cars waited at corners for regular passengers and the crews did errands in town for the neighbors along the way. Railroading, too, was once a country affair, innocent of the grim necessities of urban commerce as was the national spirit of the times, and to many this charm and flavor has never entirely been lost amid the urgency of a latter industrial age.

By no means, however, can this sentimental nostalgia, which every person of sensibilities experiences toward some aspect of the past, obscure the fascination of railroading in the twentieth century, when the Pacific Coast is only as far from New York, in railroading hours, as Chicago was once. No souvenirs of shooting buffalo from Central Pacific Palace cars or breakfasting, somewhat robustly for contemporary taste, off rye whisky and waffles at early Harvey Houses can abate the glory of the City of San Francisco streaking down the far slopes of the Rockies at dawn or the fine surge of one of the R.F. & P.'s giant 4-8-4s wheeling north before a hotshot freight from the groves of Florida with a white feather at her stack and a smoke trail two miles behind to mark her going.

It is conceivable that the end is in sight for much that is picturesque and stirring to the imagination in the railroad scene. Electrification, Diesel power and the frequently fatuous devices of streamlining do not quicken the heart. Romance and glory are implicit in outside motion, in side rods, cross-heads, eccentrics and the implacable rhythm of counter-balanced driving-wheels reeling off the miles as the chapters of history were once written by the measured *passus* of the Roman legions. Railroading has become too involved and costly an enterprise to concern itself with legend and sentiment. The expenditures of the Sante Fe for a single year recently equalled the total appropriations for the same period of three states through which its iron passed. The brass-railed observation-platform, so dear to the hearts of passengers, has been supplanted by, God save us, inclosed lounges of nightmare shapes and paneled with health glass. Only along the Maine Central and a few roads in the Pacific northwest has the high-ball refused to bow to the supremacy of automatic-position light signals that are as innocent of human fallibility as they are of atmosphere. The contents of this book (your railroader would call it "consist") have been assembled to record for the author's pleasure and for amateurs of the legend some aspects of a century of transportation that the future will remember as the cycle of steam. If it can communicate to any of its readers any part of the excitement he experienced in its preparation, it will be its own justification.

To obtain some of the photographs that illustrate this book the author has traveled many thousands of miles and all of them with intense pleasure, whether it was waiting at Needles for the Grand Canyon Limited to climb against the quivering horizon, all smoke and glory and thunder, or lounging amidst the frontier souvenirs of the "Little Nugget" bar aboard the City of Los Angeles. He has ridden over the seemingly lost world of West Texas along the Southern Pacific and stalked the Sportsman as it rolled with the sleek beauty of fifteen green Pullmans off the long bridge over the Potomac and into Virginia.

The circumstance that the arrival of a given limited or hotshot freight over a given stretch of track is predestined and practically inevitable has never abated the excitement of the moment when the pilot sweeps across the camera sights, and not all trains are accommodating in the matter of daylight runs, smoke effects or suitable backgrounds. Heavy smoke clouds pouring from a locomotive are frowned upon by railroad men as both inefficient operation and bad promotion and yet they are one of the photographer's few recordable indexes of speed and action. In the case of backgrounds most train photographers feel that a certain degree of representative country-side should be associated with a train shot as typical of its run, so that a picture, say, of the Daylight against the California hillslopes or the Empire State Express beside the Hudson has a rightness about it that is complementary to the dominant importance of the locomotive and train itself.

There are, to be sure, railroad "amateurs" like Raymond Loewy and

Henry Dreyfuss, each of them distinguished industrial designers, to whose esthetic senses the air-stream pattern of ultimate modernity is more satisfying than the visible mechanical details of eccentrics and air-pumps, feed water-heaters, hand-rails and sand domes. Their creed of locomotive design includes the abatement of rivet heads and visible detail of construction in favor of built-in smoke deflectors, front end air-foil formation, the blending of engine cab and tender and the fairing-in of car trucks. Within certain limits the streamlining of train equipment is esthetically justifiable. Its judicious practice has furnished the Southern Pacific's Daylight, perhaps the most beautiful of all train designs, the new Twentieth Century Limited, the Texas and New Orleans' Sunbeams and the New Haven's "Shoreliners" of the 1,400 class.

When it comes to the designs of Diesel power, however, most rail enthusiasts, and especially the photographic-minded among them, are baffled and saddened. There is nothing significant of action in the passing of the Denver Zephyr except an *envoi* in the form of a cloud of dust and the corpse of an occasional chicken immolated on the altar of speed, and nothing so cheers the traditionalist as the spectacle of the Super Chief being assisted up the hillsides by one of the Santa Fe's Northerns, all guts and exhibitionism and smoke, for all the world like a 1910 Pope Hartford trailing shamefully home behind a team of plow horses. There is a wonder and a beauty to the City of Los Angeles but there is not motion and there is not the stirring thunder of exhaust.

Many people have been helpful to the author in the preparation of this book, some of them executives, notably in the offices of the Southern Pacific, the Frisco and the New York Central, but largely he is indebted to amateurs of railroading rather than participants in its mysteries. To H. W. Pontin of Railroad Photographs and G. M. Best, who are, perhaps, the ranking locomotive photographers of their generation, and to Gilbert Burck of the Munsey Publications, who has handsomely abetted the entire enterprise, the author is much in debt. To all and any who may share his own vast and urgent enthusiasm for the magnificence of power and wheels and rails these pages are commended and dedicated.

L. B.

1   "O PIONEERS"

FEW words in the American lexicon possess such power to lay hold upon the imagination as "Union Pacific." The names of events and places and heroes and battles, the hall-marks of faiths and oriflammes of causes cannot shake the heart and clutch at the imagining as does the legend of the valiant and ineffable West and of the men and the railroad that brought it into being and fulfilment. For the West is America, and once, when all the world was young, Union Pacific was the West.

To the enlightened imagination, Union Pacific does not mean only the right of way and rails, the power and rolling-stock, the structure and invested economy of an operating company best known for a stretch of steel running from Omaha to Ogden; it stands for the whole epic of a national youth, for the color and movement of only yesterday's drama, for the frontier legend of a people removed but by a single generation from the necessities of desert and wilderness, and for a coda to this theme written in terms of ultimate and luxurious modernity.

In the name Union Pacific are conquest and commerce, destiny and dynasties, the essence of a nation, young, tough, blasphemous, prodigal, with the future ahead of it, and triumphant and quite invincible at the hands of any circumstance. In the beginning the wonderful West lay beyond the rail-head. More seductive than the Medford rum and the fiddles playing "Clementine" in the first-and-last-chance saloons of Iowa border towns, more urgent than the raffish and rapacious madams and the maidens of mirth that followed the iron across the continent, the desert and the sunset called men from the salmon weirs and down-land meadows of the Kennebec, from the feuds and ballad English of the Kentucky mountains, but not from the Sharps rifles. The Sharps rifles went west, too.

Union Pacific is one of three railroad empires that hold in fief all that is west of the Mississippi. It was, before that, a pageant of stupendous achievement, of Stevens-built eight-wheelers and men of imagination, appetite for action and indomitable perseverance. Its movement was laid against the Nebraska corn-fields, the grim and saline marches of Utah, and it was orchestrated to gun-fire, the heart-of-oak songs of County Mayo and the ageless clatter of minted gold in the counting-houses of Sacramento and State Street. Never before or since has America heard so surgent a symphony as drifted downwind from the North Platte and Cheyenne, from Rawlins and Bitter Creek and the slopes of the Wasatch.

Agitation for a railroad running from the Atlantic seaboard to the Pacific coast began to make itself heard as early as the year 1832, when the Baltimore and Ohio had been chartered for less than half a decade and there were only 140 miles of strap iron rails laid in the entire United States. Seers and visionaries foresaw even in the middle thirties the day when the iron highroad should stretch, by vague and various routings to be sure, but none the less certainly, from Ohio to Oregon. For twenty-odd years, while conservative men of affairs doubted if the railroad was actually here to stay—although venturing occasional and hair-raising business trips on the "train brigades" of the Philadelphia and Columbia or the Germantown and Norristown—there were mutterings of a Pacific Railroad in the halls of Congress and the columns of a reckless popular press. It was not until 1853 that, at the command of Congress, Secretary of War Jefferson Davis directed five corps of United States Engineers "to ascertain the most practicable and economical route for a railroad from the Mississippi River to the Pacific Ocean."

It is not purposed here to retell the story of the Union and Central Pacific construction—a theme which has engaged reporters, historians and novelists, moralists, economists and even the authors of ballets—so much as briefly to trace some of the dramatic overtones of the progress of the rails and the men who laid them high above the waters of the American River in the Sierras, across the arms of the North Platte and down the western slopes of the Wasatch, and into the fertile valley of the Latter-day Saints.

In point of actual fact the project and its realization which were known to the sixties as the Pacific Railroad were two quite separate undertakings, originated, financed and directed by different groups in widely divergent parts of the continent and only assuming a common continuity upon their point of unification to form a continuous iron highway between Omaha and the Pacific coast. The Central Pacific Railroad, to-day an integral part of the system known as the Southern Pacific Lines, started at Sacramento and worked eastward over the High Sierras, across the entire width of Nevada and into Utah as far as the junction point of Promontory. Union Pacific had its source of origin at Omaha and its construction ran westward across Nebraska and Wyoming as far as Ogden, Utah, from where its rails eventually continued north and west around the margins of the Great Salt Lake to the point just east of Monument Rock known as Promontory, where it joined the Central. Linking Omaha with Chicago and the East, but built entirely independently of either the Central or the Union Pacific, was the Chicago and North Western Railroad whose actual terminus was at Council Bluffs, Iowa, on the eastern shore of the Missouri River, but whose trains, as a matter of common convenience, actually are taken over by the Union Pacific in Omaha itself.

Of the two great works of track-laying which progressed toward each other as the Central Pacific on the west and Union Pacific in the east to meet, quite unpredictably, at Promontory on a spring morning in 1869, the Central was at once the first to get under way, the more orderly in its progress and less subject to criticism on grounds of financial irregularities. Union Pacific was a dissolute, hugger-mugger venture by comparison, the source and fountainhead of the doubtless reprehensible but still vaguely humorous Credit Mobilier "scandal," howling and shooting its way westward against all the laws of propriety and probability. The tumult which accompanied the Union's progress by no means detracted from the spaciousness and grandeur of vision which characterized the enterprise nor from the heroic aspects of its accomplishment; rather they added to it a flavor of Americanism and the old West which is to cling to its memory forever.

The Central Pacific had come into being in 1861 under the guidance of Leland Stanford, California's wartime governor, Mark Hopkins, an Argonaut and conservative Sacramento business man, Collis Potter Huntington, a Connecticut Yankee and partner with Hopkins in retailing hardware and miners' supplies (even as, in distant Massachusetts, Oakes and Oliver Ames were manufacturers of shovels and agricultural tools), and Charles Crocker, Sacramento's leading dry-goods merchant. Associated with these mining-land magnates were Edwin, Charles Crocker's brother and the first of many resourceful attorneys for the Central and later the Southern Pacific, Aaron Sargent, the company's Washington agent, and Theodore Judah, who had built California's first railroad from Sacramento to Folsom and who was to become chief engineer for the Central and one of the most celebrated names in the annals of railroad construction in America.

The lure, and it was a glittering one, at the Central's inception, was the trade of the newly discovered Nevada silver mines. As a link in the transcontinental road no one at first thought of it. California's El Dorado was paling by comparison with the sheen of Nevada's Silverado and, in the midst of the already crescent excitement, hysteria was precipitated by the discovery of the unbelievable Comstock Lode. Virginia City was baptized with a flagon of forty-rod whisky, and the stage lines of Wells Fargo and Company were hiring extra shot-gun messengers for their swaying Concord coaches between Virginia City and Placerville. To ferry the bulk of these fabulous transactions into Sacramento by railroad promised a net of anything one wanted to imagine, starting at a basic certainty of $5,000,000 yearly. If they had to cast the rails the whole way in polished silver it seemed a bet not to be missed.

There was a vast deal of opposition to the railroad. The stage companies saw in iron rails the handwriting on the wall, and the California,

Overland and Pioneer companies banded to halt the undertaking. So did the Overland Telegraph, whose wires now stretched from Placerville to Salt Lake City, and there tagged along a legion of wagoners, freight contractors and expressmen. "Whispering campaigns," conducted in stentorian tones in saloons and counting-houses, pilloried it as "the Dutch Flat Swindle" from the name of the proposed route. The Central was beset with such financial difficulties and harassments that at one time there was no money at all in its treasury for seventeen days.

But what the industry and determination of Huntington and Crocker seemed unable to achieve was accomplished by the progress of the Civil War. Communication with California, the transportation of its wealth eastward in the interests of the Union cause, and the menace of the Confederacy along the long-considered southern route for the Pacific Railroad all expedited the selection of the alternate line of construction westward from Omaha and hastened the appropriation by Congress of assistance in the form of land grants for the company undertaking the work. Like the Central, the Union was undertaken on private capital, but, unlike the Central, which was chartered to conduct its affairs within the state of California and only came under the guidance of national legislation after it had crossed into Nevada, the Union Pacific was from its inception operated under a Federal charter.

The personnel of the Union was almost as predominantly eastern as that of the Central was Californian. The great banks of issue of the era were located in Boston rather than, as later, in New York and the brothers Oakes and Oliver Ames of the famed Massachusetts family became its financial geniuses. Leagued with them in New York where the main offices of the enterprise were located was Dr. Thomas C. Durant, builder of the Mississippi and Missouri Railroad in Iowa, Sidney Dillon, a New Yorker, whose beginnings had been with the Albany and Schenectady Railroad, General Jack Casement and his brother Dan T. Casement, and General Grenville M. Dodge who, at the age of thirty-five, in 1866 became the chief engineer of the road. Colonel Silas Seymour of New York was appointed consulting engineer to General Dodge; Samuel B. Reed was superintendent of construction, and the divisional chiefs included Thomas H. Bates, James A. Evans, F. M. Case, Percy L. Browne and

L. L. Hills, both of whom were killed by Indians in the course of progress westward, J. E. House, Marshall F. Hurd, F. C. Hodges, James R. Maxwell, John O'Neill, Francis Appleton, J. O. Hudnut, J. F. McCabe, Jacob Blickensderfer, Jr., and Thomas B. Morris. David Van Lennep of the New York School of Mines was geologist for the road and the Government directors were headed by Jesse L. Williams, an Indiana engineer of competence and more than usually expert knowledge of his field.

Even with the assistance of the Federal Government, largely moral and in the form of promises of land grants, and later in cash bonuses based on construction, the Union experienced almost overwhelming difficulties in getting under way. At a meeting of stockholders in 1863, thirty directors and officers were chosen, and two months later land was first broken at the sprawling frontier village of Omaha, but at the close of the first year of actual construction only 40 miles of road had been graded and that at a cost of $1,000,000, leaving the treasury practically empty. Eastern capital was slow to respond, and it was not until July, 1865, that, at Omaha, the first rail was laid, the first spike driven and the endless iron started stretching out over the waiting grades.

It was here that there became first discernible to the ear the stirring rhythm of the westering march of the rail-layers. Until now the strophe had been sounded in muted and dubious key, in the grimy corridors of Washington, in the high studded offices of Sidney Dillon in New York, in gas-lit private rooms in Parker's looking across wintry School Street to King's Chapel in Boston. Now the antistrophe grew, strong and tumultuous, above the downland reaches of the Platte. Union Pacific, sensing at its roots, deep driven half-way across the continent into the treasure-houses of the east, a new flow of vitality, surged with sudden life. Brick engine houses and machine-shops, an immense carriage house, tool shops and nearly six hundred less pretentious dwellings sprang up in Omaha. A single business block given over to offices and counting-houses cost $100,000. Grocery houses of hitherto modest proportions were doing a gross of $500,000 annually. Four locomotives, twenty-seven passenger-coaches and a vast number of box-cars and flats arrived by river steamer from St. Louis. A 70-ton stationary engine was hauled by ox teams across western Iowa and lightered across the river in defiance of probability and the opinions of the skeptical. One million ties were piled and ready to start for the advancing rail-head as they might be needed. Life boiled and seethed in Omaha in the saloons and faro houses and lupanaria as it once had in California's El Dorado and as it would forty years later in the gelid reaches of the Yukon. The last American frontier was beginning to recede before the combined agencies of the Brothers Casement, Oliver Ames and Sons, and the established physical circumstance that water, changed to steam, occupies 1,600 times its original space. For the first time there was heard the sound, unstilled from then till now, of the boiler exhaust exploding upward through diamond stacks at Fremont, at Columbus, at Grand Island, and the ceaseless side rods commenced their progress over the 60-pound rails.

In the beginning there was North Platte, just under 300 miles out of Omaha on the Nebraska plains. From a subdued township of fewer than 500 people it flowered, within a fortnight in the fall of '66, to a bragging, swaggering urban midst inhabited by 5,000 wild Irish and their camp-followers and possessed of a roundhouse for 40 locomotives, a Railroad House Hotel that had been sent out of Chicago in knocked-down form and reassembled in a single morning, a water tank of ample size "and beautiful proportions" and a frame depot which was also esthetically satisfactory. Poker artists and roulette manipulators from as far away as New Orleans and the water-front of Natchez leaped from the river packets at St. Louis and two nights later were part of the gaudy night-life of North Platte. Houses of pretty girls, imported intact with madams and inmates from Chicago, seethed with amorous activity. Real estate speculators anticipated the latter-day follies of Florida and California, and North Platte was widely if somewhat exaggeratedly advertised as "the Paris of Nebraska."

"Every gambler in the Union seems to have steered his course for North Platte," wrote Henry M. Stanley, later of Dr. Livingstone fame. "Every house is a saloon and every saloon is a gambling den. Revolvers are in great requisition. Beardless youths imitate to the life the peculiar swagger of the devil-may-care bullwhacker and blackleg, and here, for the first time, they try their hands at Mexican monte, high-low-jack, strap, rouge-et-noire, three-card monte and that Satanic game, chuck-a-luck.... Old gamblers who revelled in the glorious days of 'flush times' in the gold districts declare that this town outstrips all yet."

More than anything else, vitality surged westward with the course of the ever-lengthening rails and in such superabundance that the working-day, from sunrise to sunset, seemed insufficient for its satisfaction and discharge. Thus it was that the so-called "roaring towns" came into being in the wake of the march from Omaha across the plains and a night-life which was at once the most abandoned, hilarious and deadly ever known in the land put to noisy shame even San Francisco's Barbary Coast and the happy howling of New York's boasted Tenderloin.

Nobody has ever tabulated the gallons of forty-rod whisky which, together with the millions of ties and hundreds of thousands of tons of rails, were consumed in laying down the U.P.'s stretch of the Pacific Railroad. The figures would probably be frightening to a generation of less heroic toss-pots and more abated thirsts, but just as elections in America have, as an inevitable by-product of enlightened democracy, been floated in rum, the U.P. floated into existence upon a tide, indeed a veritable Niagara, of strong waters. The progress of empire strewed the desert and illustrated the plains with empty flasks and the erection of a handsome and ample saloon was the first of all considerations when a new construction camp was being staked out. For Dodge's Irishmen were serious drinkers and they took incidental but considered pleasure, while pursuing their favorite sport, in howling, screaming, gouging out each other's eyes, discharging firearms and setting fire to the premises. The atmosphere of the roaring towns was somewhat less tranquil than that, say, of Arsenal Street in Springfield, Massachusetts, on a Sunday afternoon. Sam Bowles of the Springfield *Republican* called them "Hell on Wheels" but it all depends on the individual attitude.

Epic was the progress of Union Pacific and epic were the nights of North Platte and Cheyenne, of Laramie, Wasatch, Corinne and Promontory. All the world it seemed was moving west with the rail-head. The roaring towns seethed with settlers and gold seekers, professional gamblers in pearl gray top-hats with Remington derringers in their lace cuffs, cattle drovers with bull whips, engineers and construction workers in jack-boots, tradesmen, newspaper reporters, Mormons, publicans,

Courtesy of the Southern Pacific

AROUND CAPE HORN

Building the line of the Central Pacific into the Sierras, workmen were faced with the task of cutting road-beds into the geologic formation of mountains so steep that they had to be suspended by ropes 3,000 feet above the torrent of the American River on hanging stages. By the spring of 1865 the rails had been laid from Sacramento to Colfax, around Cape Horn and into Dutch Flat. Here is one of the C.P.'s first freights running double-header around Cape Horn with all three brakemen, head, swing and parlor, ready to tie them down when needed. When this photograph was taken telegraph lines had already been strung into the mountains; there were three trains a day between Colfax and Sacramento, and a short time later the road was doing a brisk hauling business between its California terminus and the mines of Nevada.

IN THE SIERRAS, 1868

Somewhere above Cisco, as the Central Pacific's Chinese blasted their way to the summit of the Sierras a year before the completion of the transcontinental railroad, an imaginative photographer poised his apparatus atop a rocking box-car to get what must be one of the earliest action photographs on record. Below is the C. P.'s Oneonta, shown wooding up at Cisco a year previous to this time.

THE YESTERDAY OF BRET HARTE

This is Palisade, Nevada, shortly after the first iron of the Central Pacific emerged from the Sierras in 1868. The Overland Telegraph lines already ran through the main street which faces on the railroad. Although such towns along the Central as Winnemucca, Argenta and Carlin boasted terminus booms as the rail-head passed them, none of the frontier towns west of Ogden save Promontory knew the "hell on wheels" which accompanied the Union Pacific's progress through Nebraska and Wyoming, with its irrepressible and triumphant turmoil. A Central town which shared in this gusty tradition was Elko during the days of the White Pine Mines boom. Another Nevada township, at first nameless, was known for its impressive bill-board which pointed the way to the principal place of business with the legend "To Bar." With the good sense of the frontier the place was named Tobar, as it stands in the *Postal Guide* to this day. Below: The Union's No. 119, Promontory protagonist, at Omaha, 1869.

ABOVE TRUCKEE IN THE SIERRAS

The Central Pacific's Chinese laborers building a fill on the descending slope as the construction approached Reno with the aid of hand-carts and mules.

IN THE SIERRAS

The technique known as angle photography is commonly supposed to be of comparatively recent professional origin. Here, however, is an angle shot dating from 1868 and showing one of the Central Pacific's woodburners, complete with balloon stack and screen covering, which ran up into the mountains from Sacramento and Dutch Flat with materials to push the rail-head eastward. As no night runs were yet inaugurated over the Sierra construction when this picture was taken, the C.P.'s No. 22 carried no headlight on the platform ahead of her smokestack. In the background is American Canyon as it appeared from Cape Horn.

ON THE CISCO–SACRAMENTO RUN, 1867

The locomotive Hercules, a 2-6-0 type, starts down out of the Sierras with a drag freight. Cisco, 15 miles above Dutch Flat and at a height of nearly 6,000 feet where the snow sometimes made construction impossible as late as May, was for nine months the terminus of the Central Pacific while engineers and labor gangs fought through to the summit of the Sierras 14 miles farther to the east. The powder bill for construction alone at this time ran to $54,000 a month with 500 kegs a day required to blast the way. But the Overland stages connected with the Central at Cisco and the freight business between Sacramento and the Nevada mines was starting to demonstrate the profitable possibilities of the road.

Courtesy of the Southern Pacific

THE U.P. TRAIL

Victory was the name given the Central Pacific camp in Nevada where the rails ended in April, 1869, after the C.P.'s Chinese had laid down ten miles of track in a single day. The man in the beard and morning coat is J. H. Strobridge, construction superintendent, and beside him H. H. Minkler, track-laying boss. Below is the single track of the Central Pacific reaching across the Humboldt.

Courtesy of the Southern Pacific

AWAITING A RENDEZVOUS WITH DESTINY

When the Union Pacific trains, laden with dignitaries from the east bound for the ceremonies at Promontory, were delayed by heavy rains in the Wasatch, Leland Stanford's train with his party of Central Pacific guests and officials retired to Monument Point siding, 30 miles west of Promontory. Here the steward contrived to shoot a mess of plover and all on board explored the surrounding landscape. This very rare photograph from the files of the Southern Pacific shows the wires of the Overland Telegraph, strung from rudely trimmed timbers, in the foreground and the Jupiter, with a good head of steam, waiting for word to return to Promontory. The tank-car, directly behind the locomotive, was of a type then carried by every train crossing the western deserts. The Jupiter was built in 1868 by Schenectady. Her drivers were 5 feet, her cylinders 16 by 24 inches, and her weight 65,450 pounds. It was raining when this photograph was taken, as is indicated by the dreary aspect of the desert surrounding the margin of the Great Salt Lake with Monument Rock visible in the background.

Blank No. 1.

0177

THE WESTERN UNION TELEGRAPH COMPANY.

The rules of this Company require that all messages received for transmission, shall be written on the message blanks of the Company, under and subject to the conditions printed thereon, which conditions have been agreed to by the sender of the following message.

THOS. T. ECKERT, Gen'l Sup't, New York.   WILLIAM ORTON, Pres't,   O. H. PALMER, Sec'y, New York.

Dated *Promontory Utah via Omaha* 186 9

Received at *May 9*

To *Oliver Ames,*

Prest.

You can make affidavit of Completion of road to Promontory Summit.

G. M. Dodge

Chf Engr

11.400 Coll

Rec May 10

THE RAIL-HEAD MOVES EAST

This wooden trestle was built by Theodore Judah's construction gangs as the Central Pacific forged up into the Sierra foot-hills at Newcastle, California, late in 1864. The 2-6-0 woodburner was displacing the classic American-type locomotive for mountain hauls, but so rapid was the construction on this line in the race to meet the iron of the Union Pacific that it was not until a decade later that, in the middle seventies, many of these precarious and vulnerable wooden trestles were converted into dirt fills or embankments by Chinese day-labor. At left: the telegram from General Dodge to Oliver Ames telling of the completion of the Union Pacific at Promontory.

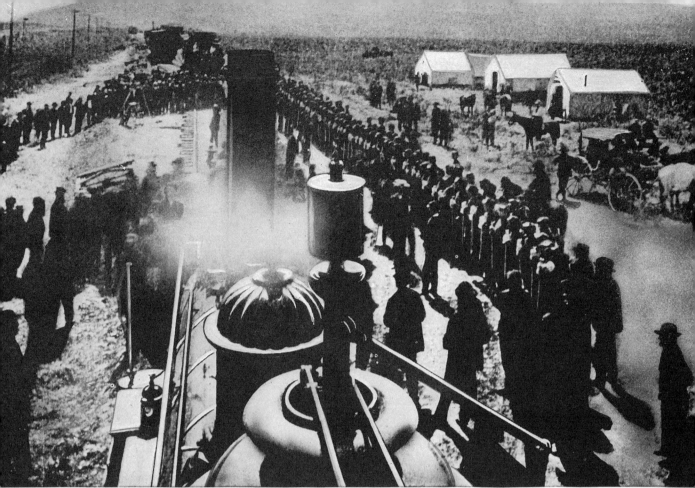

Courtesy of the Southern Pacific

RENDEZVOUS WITH DESTINY

Photographed from the cab roof of No. 119 and showing its characteristic Rogers fluted sand dome in the foreground, this is the scene at Promontory at 2:40 P.M. on May 10, five minutes before the final phase of the ceremonies which marked the completion of the Pacific Railroad. The shot was probably taken by Colonel Charles R. Savage, the empty tripod for whose camera may be seen in the left middle background. The deal table of W. N. Shilling of the Western Union is beside the track, hidden by the straight smoke-stack of No. 119. The white gauntlets of the Twenty-first Infantry, standing at rest, gleam in the sun and visible in the center of the track is Major Milton Cogswell, commanding. This is the stage as it was set for the closing scene in the most epic of all railroad dramas. Below: Behind the scenes at Promontory showing Leland Stanford's private car mentioned by breathless newspaper correspondents on the scene for the occasion as a "magnificent piece of cabinet work" after the ceremonies.

Courtesy of the Southern Pacific

Railroad Photographs

SERVING THE DESERT

Seventy years after the Jupiter and other locomotives on desert runs in the far west first hauled extra water for their boilers in tanks behind the tender, tank-cars are still part of the regular train equipment on long hauls where water is not available or that which is chemically unsuitable. Despite the changes in locomotive design, the Texas and Pacific ten-wheeler in the photograph is close kin to the first U.P. and Central Pacific engines which pulled their extra water on the desert runs in the sixties.

Courtesy of the Southern Pa

THE LAST RAIL

Promontory, 1869

Bearded track gangs of the Union and Central Pacific stand by for the ceremony which is to accompany the laying and spiking of the last rail.

JUBILATION IN MONTGOMERY STREET

The civil authorities, the military from the Presidio, the firemen in white helmets and the citizens in beaver hats, indeed almost every one in San Francisco with the possible exception of the agents of Wells, Fargo & Co., at one time or another got into the parade which, on May 8, 1869, wended its way from Kearny to Washington and then down Montgomery after a tumultuous start from the saloons adjacent to Portsmouth Square. The Sather Bank is the building in the right center at the corner of Commercial and Montgomery. The *Dramatic Chronicle* was the celebrated DeYoung property before it became the daily San Francisco *Chronicle* of the present time The celebration lasted for three full days.

Courtesy of Railroad Magazine

LUXURIES OF PALACE-CAR TRAVEL

Just a year after the driving of the final spike at Promontory the Boston Board of Trade, its families and guests embarked on a specially designed train of eight "of the most elegant cars ever drawn over an American railroad" for a through trip to San Francisco and the golden wonders of the newly opened West. The two Pullman hotel-cars, "Arlington" and "Revere," were equipped with "well-stocked libraries replete with choice works of fiction, history, poetry, etc., and two of the improved Burdett organs...complete in every detail of stops, pedals, double banks of keys, etc." Culture, the humanities and, possibly, the comforting qualities of faith are represented in this contemporary drawing from "The Pacific Tourist—Williams' Illustrated Trans-Continental Guide of Travel" where the noble red man joins his white brother, the one in Navajo attire, the other in Prince Albert and Dundrearies, to sing hymns of a Sunday evening while crossing the plains.

BACK HEAD, 1869

This is the machinery which confronted the hogger in the decade after the Civil War: Johnson bar, throttle, main feed-valve and boiler-pressure gage. Driving a locomotive was simpler then.

Upper right: Courte
of the Southern P

BIRTHPLACE OF A DREAM OF EMPIRE

Over this emporium of wheelbarrows, pickaxes, powder and fuse, at the time this sketch was made immortality and fortune, more or less unsuspected, hovered for Collis P. Huntington, Mark Hopkins, Theodore Judah, Leland Stanford and Charles Crocker. For on June 28, 1861, at the hardware store of Huntington, Hopkins and Company, 54 K Street, Sacramento, the Central Pacific Railroad Company of California, capitalized at 85,000 shares, par value $100, was incorporated under the laws of the state. Fame for Theodore Judah, chief construction engineer of the Central Pacific, was to be posthumous, since he died in the midst of his labors two years later.

Lower right: courte
the Southern Pacifi

HUNTINGTON HOPKINS & CO.
54 K
ESTABLISHED 1850.

NAILS, SHOVELS, PICKS, HANDLES, WHEEL BARROWS, GAS PIPE & FITTINGS, RUBBER HOSE, BELTING, POWDER, FUSE, ROPE, BLOCKS, PITCH, TAR

OFFICE

HUNTINGTON
HOPKINS & CO
HARDWARE

WESTWARD COURSE OF EMPIRE

On the Wyoming plains, west of Cheyenne, the Casement brothers pushed the U.P. rail-head with 10,000 Irish graders and track-layers. During the winter of 1868 vast stores of timber, ties and rails had been massed in Cheyenne warehouses and the photograph shows a supply train, triple-headed, pushing up behind the construction gangs. Civilization followed the iron with various conflicting manifestations. In Cheyenne so great was the uproar of frontier night-life, populated by gamblers, shady political colonels, bullwhackers, pimps, prostitutes and madams, Mexicans, Indians, half-breeds, gunmen, saloon proprietors and ex-soldiers that the Vigilance Committee had to hang a dozen or so low characters before the turmoil abated. In the Episcopal Diocese of Nebraska at the same period fourteen new churches were erected in as many townships.

GRANDFATHER LOOKED AND VOYAGED THUS

Substantially attired in stock collar, frock-coat, Albert watch-chain and Masonic emblem, this side-whiskered gentleman of the year '69 is braving the perils of rail travel, Indians and outlaws aboard one of the first transcontinental trains run through by the Central Pacific. In his Gladstone bag the chances are he carried a copy of Young's *Night Thoughts,* a flannel nightshirt, a Colt's Navy revolver and a leather-cased flask of Sherwood whisky. Thus armed against all emergencies, he might travel in considerable comfort and tolerable speed from Sacramento to Chicago in this Silver Palace type car, the design and principle of which were taken over by George Pullman's company in 1883.

SUPER-POWER IN THE SIXTIES

This 4-6-0 locomotive, designed for mountain hauls on the Central Pacific, was built by McKay and Aldus in 1866. A giant for its time, its drivers were 4 feet 6 inches, its cylinders 18 by 24, and it weighed 73,000 pounds. The Auburn was No. 22 on the C.P. roster. Notice, too, the ornamental decoration engrossed on the side panel of the headlight in an age when the engineers rather than the railroads often owned engine headlights.

Courtesy of the Southern Pacific

TRACK INSPECTION, 1869

Before the inauguration of track-inspection cars or locomotives with glassed-in observation-cabs for this purpose, these United States Commissioners rode over the Central Pacific's newly laid iron at Argenta, Nevada, wrapped in buffalo-robes atop the cow-catcher of the Falcon. In contrast to the pioneer simplicity of buffalo-robes and a sleigh seat on the cow-catcher, this Chicago, Burlington and Quincy American-type locomotive has been rebuilt with an elaborate glassed-in cab for the convenience of track inspection and official tours of the road.

Railroad Photographs

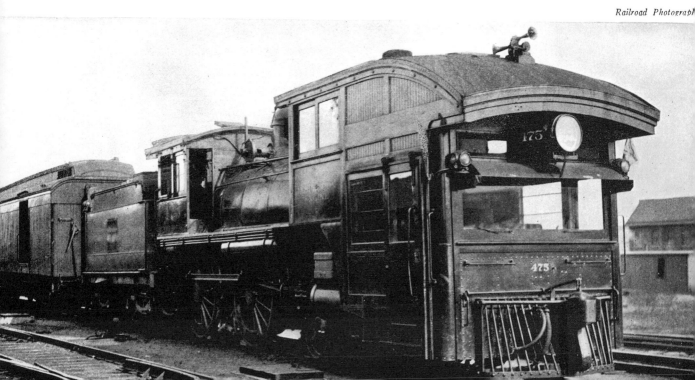

"BLESS ME, THIS IS PLEASANT, RIDING ON THE RAIL!"

Better, perhaps, than any railroading picture of the era, this wet plate photograph of a New York, New Haven and Hartford American-type 4-4-0 locomotive rolling out of Meriden, Connecticut, in 1882 which had to be developed by the photographer within a few moments of exposure, captures the atmosphere of the times. It caught the engineer's straw hat, the Dreyfuss self-feeding oil cups on the side rods, the polished brass of the smoke-stack and the fine, oily sheen of soft coal smoke billowing downwind. It is one of the first and at the same time one of the finest of all railroad action shots.

eastern financiers, strumpets, jobbers, soldiers, rufflers and shady political colonels. Englishmen in deer-stalker caps and Inverness cloaks of outrageous pattern came out to see what was toward and returned to tell
their countrymen that Americans were forever shooting each other at
table and that every one in the States drank a quart of whisky before
breakfast. Newspapermen were swamped with the most magnificent and
colorful copy of the century. Snake-oil vendors shouted their sovereign
cures from wagon tails at every corner. Firearms dealers disposed of
Colt's Frontier model .45's and Starr's Navy Revolvers of wall-piece
dimensions by the carload lot. Hallowe'en at the madhouse assumed a
sylvan tranquillity by comparison.

Over all this tumult of achievement, vitality, remorseless labor and
Dionysiac relaxation stood the Casement brothers. General Jack Casement had seen service in the war and such a scene was the familiar
breath of life to him. Nine out of ten of the men working on the Union
Pacific had fought either in the Union or the Confederate army and
Casement, five feet of bearded and frock-coated toughness, dominated
them as he had dominated his Ohio troops a few years before.

In May, 1867, the U.P. trail established as its base of operations Julesburg, Colorado, 377 miles out of Omaha, and proud to advertise itself
as "the wickedest city in America." Once known as Canvastown, Julesburg was more enduringly named for a French trapper who had, in a
moment of marital pique, murdered his wife, and the town did all it
could to justify its name. When the U.P. was still wintering in North
Platte, Julesburg boasted a population, typical of the frontier times, of
forty men and one woman. By July there were 4,000 in its streets, and
the proportion of females had been vastly improved. Portable frame
buildings went up in a morning. There were dwellings, stores, machine
shops, hotels, refectories and what one dainty-minded historian described
as "recreatories." There were soldiers, gamblers, Indians, railroad boom-
ers, land speculators, Mexicans, evangelists, ranchers, prostitutes and
all the other accustomed camp-followers. There were dog fights in the
dusty streets, gun fights in the saloons, hair-pullings and gougings among
the girls and sluggings beyond counting at the faro tables. The joy of
living assumed positively gladiatorial proportions and the inanimate

clay was off to Boot Hill, the local graveyard where victims of gun-play were buried in their riding-boots, every morning before the carrousels had stopped playing or the kerosene flares were extinguished in the gaming-tents.

A mixed crowd, composed of gamblers, teamsters, and soldiers, greeted us [wrote Stanley], all of whom were eager and anxious for news. Bustling through them, I found my way to the very comfortable quarters at the Jules-burg House, and was fortunate enough to find a feast composed of various styles of soups, *fricandeaux,* vegetables, game in abundance, pies, puddings, raisins, apples, nuts, wine and bread at *discretion,* for the moderate sum of twelve bits. I was astonished to find such company as then and there sat at table. Everybody had gold watches attached to expensive chains, and was dressed in well-made clothes, and several wore patent leather boots. I vow I thought these were great capitalists, but was astonished to find they were only clerks, ticket agents, conductors, engineers, and "sich like." These *habitués* of the Julesburg House were the upper-ten-dom of sinful Jules-burg. . . .

The women are expensive articles, and come in for a large share of the money wasted. In broad daylight they may be seen gliding through the sandy streets in Black Crook dresses, carrying fancy derringers slung to their waists, with which tools they are dangerously expert. Should they get into a fuss, western chivalry will not allow them to be abused by any man whom they may have robbed.

At night new aspects are presented in this city of premature growth. Watch-fires gleam over the sea-like expanse of ground outside of the city, while inside soldiers, herdsmen, teamsters, women, railroad men, are dancing, singing or gambling. I verily believe that there are men here who would murder a fellow-creature for five dollars. Nay, there are men who have already done it, and who stalk abroad in daylight unwhipped of justice. Not a day passes but a dead body is found somewhere in the vicinity with pockets rifled of their con-tents. But the people generally are strangely indifferent to what is going on.

Fun was fun in sinful Julesburg and General Casement was nobody to stop the boys from having a good time within limits. If they would confine their activities, he let it be known, to getting falling-down drunk at night and shooting out the lights in moments of excessive abandon, nobody would say a word against it, but it soon became apparent that the blacklegs, gamblers and professional gunmen meant to take over the town in its entirety without so much as a tip of the hat in the direction of Union Pacific authority. Half his track force was incapacitated every morning and they lost their pay with a dispatch and certainty unaccustomed even in a time of wholesale crookedness at the tables. It was apparent that the railroad was rapidly becoming a secondary consideration in Julesburg.

General Jack was grieved but undismayed. Upon authority from General Dodge, then prospecting the line near Salt Lake, an issue of Springfield rifles was broken open to the track forces then working a few miles out of Julesburg, and one fine summer night something very closely approximating law descended upon the town. Sin, General Jack announced, could leave within the hour. A train back to Omaha would accommodate those who had no horses. Was there any one who would care to dispute the issue? There were some who did and almost immediately it became apparent that there was an alarming shortage of lamp-posts in the town. The poles of the Overland Telegraph were found, however, suitable to serve in an emergency and in the morning the Vigilantes cut down thirty or forty who had been so injudicious as to doubt the authority of Union Pacific and removed them to Boot Hill with a minimum of ceremony.

When General Dodge returned to Julesburg a few weeks later he inquired for the whereabouts of various notorious characters who had been romping and stomping when he had passed through Julesburg before. General Jack took him on a tour of inspection to Boot Hill.

Next on the docket was Cheyenne, then pronounced "Chienna" after the Indian, 140 miles on into the dusty and wonderful West. It was already a going concern before the Union Pacific came, and when the rail-head pushed its way into the town limits all the first citizens were there to welcome it, attired in a multiplicity of Albert watch-chains and beaver hats and fairly awash with oratory and ten barrels of municipal rye. A contemporary reported that, as the crowd was milling about the platform of the new station, a long freight train drew in, laden with frame-houses, boards, furniture, palings, old tents and all the raffish and combustible essentials of one of those frontier mushroom towns. The brakeman swung down from a car top and, seeing some friends on the platform, called out with a flourish:

"Gentlemen, here's Julesburg!"

That civilization followed the rail was almost immediately demonstrated in Cheyenne. Within three weeks of the arrival of the rail-head the first newspaper commenced publication, a standing head on its front page devoted to "Last Night's Shootings." A few days after this the first authentic murder was reported, committed by a brace of scoundrels named Duggan and Howard...the victim, a U.P. grader...the time, pay-day...the cause, whisky. In November there was a magnificent prize-fight for a purse of $1,000 in gold between John Hardy and John Shaughnessy, a heroic occasion which lasted 126 rounds and which was widely heralded before and (what was remarkable) afterwards as "the most honest fight in history"!

Money was plentiful [wrote Fulton]. The company was spending vast sums to expedite construction, paying the highest prices for both labor and materials, and the money was scattered among all classes. Every known form of gambling crowded the tables in fandango houses and saloons day and night. Immense tents, each with a long bar on one side, kept open house for everybody, with bands of music blaring dance tunes for men and women, whose only admission fee was the dollar which dropped into the till as the couples lined up and took a drink after every dance, the man paying for his partner and himself at fifty cents per.

Cheyenne was built and patterned to its needs. The post-office was 10 feet by 15; the Headquarters Saloon 36 by 100. Two two-story hotels, the construction of which was finished in something less than a day, boiled with the *chic* of frontier society. A newspaper paragrapher favorable to the interests of the Rollins House reported "Chief Spotted Tail and Mrs. Spotted Tail in our midst." Magistrate Murrin impartially fined all who drew gun from holster "whether he hit or missed" at the flat rate of $10 a shooting.

"You are fined $10 and two bits."

"What's the two bits for, your honor?"

"To buy the honorable court a drink in the morning."

As at sinful Julesburg, the godless got out of hand in Cheyenne, once more mistakenly believing Union Pacific to be nothing but a combination bonanza and barbecue for the hoodlums of the continent. Lots were claimed by squatters, land-jumping became the order of the day and the military eventually marched in from Fort Russell, stretched a few necks and left Cheyenne in better shape than they had found it.

In greater measure or less, Laramie, Benton, Rawlins, Green River City, Bryan and Wasatch shared the whirlwind brevity of the rail-head life of Julesburg and Cheyenne. The touts, the tarts and the teamsters, the faro bank, rondo-coolo, keno and chuck-a-luck, the Casement brothers' portable warehouse, eating-house and general store, the gun-fire and the gouging, the hot breath, the vivid life, the quick, convulsive death and the inevitable arrival of the Vigilantes: the pattern was the same, only the locale was ever farther westward. Corinne flourished as "the Chicago of the Rocky Mountains." Nineteen saloons, two dance houses and eighty *nymphes du pavé* flourished bravely for the regulation three months.

"Yet it was withal a quiet and rather orderly place," wrote Beadle. "Sundays were generally observed; most of the men went hunting or fishing and the 'girls' had a dance or got drunk."

During the progress westward of the "Hell on Wheels" of Editor Bowles', no such epic convulsions marked the eastward march of Stanford's and Crocker's peace-loving Chinamen. For the Oriental, whisky was possessed of no compelling charm, nor were women and music upon

stringed instruments the natural complements to a day of toil. He gambled handsomely, to be sure, but with his own countrymen and his games of chance made three-card monte and faro seem by comparison about as sophisticated as pitch-penny. The Central Pacific had upon its payroll, to be sure, a number of Irishmen quite the equal in capacity for tumult and strong waters of the Union's hearts of oak, but their numbers were fewer and their enthusiasm was kept in check.

"One reason for our success was the absence of the saloon," said a Central Pacific executive after it was all over. "Don't ask me how we kept them out.... We were away by ourselves, far from courts and sheriffs, and it was remarkable that our men were so orderly and so uniformly opposed to immoral resorts. Saloons were torn down and burned by unknown hands many times, but the culprits were never discovered. A saloon would spring up in a tent once in a while, when a crowd would rush it and break bottles and heads with their pick handles, and the good red liquor would run like rain (with Superintendent Strobridge nowhere in sight)."

Truckee, Reno, Winnemucca, Carlin and Elko had their day as "roaring towns" but the construction of the Central was not the main incentive to this end. Elko, in particular, where to-day the two principal oases are modernist taverns with Venetian blinds known as the Rendezvous and the Town House, was a glad resort of the boys bent on ringing 'em and swinging 'em, but its clientele derived from the mines which illustrated the surrounding country-side rather than from the railroad. Carlin— where the City of San Francisco pauses briefly in the dark before streaking up into the Sierras, where an amiable row of bars solicit patronage with the sign "All White Help" and there is a pleasant disregard for Rule G on the part of the night trick in the dispatcher's office—had its share of enthusiastic frontier existence, but it was almost wholly divorced from the passage of the racing rail-head.

Last of all the roaring towns came Promontory, widowed to-day of traffic by the Lucin cut-off, but once a meeting place of empires where the marches of the Union Pacific and Central Pacific joined and where, for a day in May, 1869, the eyes of all America were turned. The last of the U.P. towns was part of all that its predecessors had been, raffish, brawling, diffused and unsightly, but possessed of a frontier fragrance which even to-day clings to the desert outposts of the West. For a day Promontory was to be the center of a world's attentions and that alone justified its single street, knee-deep in alkali dust and blowing tumble-weeds, its wood and canvas structures with their false fronts and the archaic, meretricious lettering announcing the "Club House" and "Pacific Hotel." One dwelling alone, Rae noted, boasted neatly arranged muslin curtains in its windows and was innocent of business bush or shingle. The strumpets ("soiled doves" was the phrase of the day) stayed on to the end. Drinking water was brought by rail from a creek eight miles distant and cost $2 a barrel. Since nobody bathed and few believed it had any future as a beverage, it was one of the commodities in which no profiteering is recorded. There were plenty of saloons but only one roulette parlor, adequate index that the U.P. treasury was at low ebb and pay-rolls a fortnight overdue. For its size, Beadle asserted, Promontory was the "nearest to the infernal regions of any town along the road," but the choruses and gun-fire are less audible down the years, the tumult obscured by the greater drama of the meeting rails.

By March of '69 the dispute for dominance of the last few miles of rail in Utah had become a knock-down fight between the Central and the Union. Between Promontory and Ogden, before either line was able to lay rails, the rival graders were blasting and filling within a few yards of each other, the one working east, the other west, in a final effort to capture the mileage and bonuses of this ultimate stretch. The U.P. survey extended to the California line, the Central's far past Ogden on into the foot-hills of the Wasatch. Neither were ready to call a halt, but in the end the Union had spent the last dollar that Oakes Ames, through any expedient of financing whatsoever, could raise. Almost at the point of economic exhaustion Vice-Presidents Huntington and Durant came to an agreement. The common terminus of the roads should be at or near Ogden. The Union Pacific should build, and the Central pay for and own, the rails from Ogden to Promontory Point were the rails were to meet and the Pacific Railroad become a completed reality.

Like the Homeric hosts before Troy, the two armies drew apart and rested on their weapons. Crocker had won his $10,000 wager with Durant, demonstrating that his Chinese rail-laying gangs could join and spike ten miles of iron between sun-up and sunset and shrewdly leaving only three miles of line to be laid to the finish so that Casement's Paddies might have no opportunity to top his record. Promontory resounded with its last nocturnal convulsions as graders and teamsters, as yet unpaid, awaited their wages from the East and drank and ate on the cuff. In San Francisco President Stanford ordered his superintendent's car stocked with ample provisions, not neglecting a quantity of champagne in magnums, and invited Chief Justice Sanderson, Governor Safford of Arizona, Collector Gates of Nevada and the three Federal Commissioners, Sherman, Haines and Trittle, for the first Central Pacific junket since construction had started out of Sacramento in 1863. The austerity which characterized the progress of Central Pacific into the Sierras and across the Humboldt desert had extended from China boy to the highest executive, but now there seemed adequate excuse for jollification. Ahead of the Stanford Special at 6:00 in the morning the regular passenger train pulled out of Sacramento, heading east with a load of sight-seers and professional Californians, a race apart which was even then making itself master of superlatives and determined to yield to no one so much as a single point in any matter of local patriotism. In the High Sierras the Stanford Special struck a felled tree that caused some delay, and it was necessary to wire on to Wadsworth to hold the regular varnish until the president's car could be attached to it for the last lap of the journey down the mountains.

The Central executives might have been delayed even longer, however, as they arrived at Promontory on the afternoon of May seventh to discover that the trains bearing Union Pacific dignitaries from Chicago had been held up by heavy rainfalls east of Ogden and that the final ceremonies could not be held until Monday, the tenth. President Stanford at once telegraphed back to California in an effort to abate the impending celebrations which he knew were planned in San Francisco and Sacramento, but too late. Already the boisterous chivalry of those communities had embarked upon a turbulent sea of oratory and slick-haired barkeeps were setting them up in schooners along the deadfalls of Geary Street. The circumstance that the festivities at Promontory were postponed for three days was hailed with universal approbation. Extra waiters were recruited in a score of restaurants; livery-stables foresaw illimitable vistas of parades and consequent custom for their best barouches, and San Francisco settled down to three days of cheering and screaming which was not to be paralleled until the turn of the century when Addison Mizner was to arrive home from Alaska coincidentally with the return of the California regiments from the Spanish War.

Monday, however, dawned clear and cold upon Promontory's great and, indeed, its almost unique day. During the night a Union Pacific construction gang had laid a full-length siding and house track down the main street, thus claiming Promontory for a U.P. terminal point and to some extent avenging the $10,000 that Vice-President Durant had lost to the Central's track-layers. The frozen mud in the streets was churned by a thousand hobnailed boots. The multiple saloons and the single gambling hell bulged till the knock-down walls threatened to part from the ready-assembled roofs sent out by Chicago mail-order houses. Where the construction was of canvas, fabric parted as did various tent ropes, and here and there a whole pavilion descended around the indifferent ears of the celebrants within. In their various Palace cars the side-whiskered executives were running lures over their beaver hats and taking precautions against the cold out of square Medford rum bottles.

Of the two ceremonial trains participating in the final rites, Vice-President Huntington's and Superintendent Crocker's, hauled by the Jupiter, was the first on the scene. An hour later the Union Pacific special, powered by Locomotive No. 119, a Rogers-built eight-wheeler, and dominated by the Durant Pullman finished in polished walnut came into view from Ogden. The eastern notables included Sidney Dillon, the Casement brothers, General Dodge, Consulting Engineer Silas Seymour, the Reverend John Todd of Pittsfield, Massachusetts, braving the perils of the fierce and bawdy West to bring Christian grace to the occasion and a number of photographers, pen and ink sketchers and newspaper correspondents. There were also four companies of the Twenty-first

Infantry under Major Milton Cogswell, and the headquarters band.

Missing from the scene were Superintendent Crocker, who was detained at Sacramento, Oakes Ames, whose absence was never satisfactorily explained, and the Mormon saint, Brigham Young, who could not lend his entire approbation to a project that had omitted Salt Lake City from its calculations and who was next week to break ground for his own Utah Central road. Conspicuously present, however, were the reporters and photographers, whose ranks included newswriters from the New York *Tribune,* Boston *Transcript,* the Springfield *Republican,* the Omaha *Herald,* San Francisco *Chronicle,* Sacramento *Press,* Chicago *Tribune* and Associated Press. Colonel Charles R. Savage was official cameraman for the occasion and his shots, many of them surprisingly modern in their angle and approach, immortalized the scene and its participants.

A chill wind blew in from the Great Salt Lake, ruffling the whiskers of the dignitaries and carrying away the shrill whistles of the locomotives converging upon the scene from east and west. Western Union Superintendent W. B. Hibbard of the Ogden office tested his wire to Omaha where circuits were being plugged in to carry his messages to New York, Washington and even to New Orleans. Westward the looping copper flowed over the insulators across the Humboldt, to Reno, to Truckee and over the passes of the High Sierras where the snow still lingered in the canyons, down to Sacramento and San Francisco where the celebration was already three days old but still unabated. Sidney Dillon later guessed there were half a thousand persons present and the photographs tend to bear out his estimate although more fervent enthusiasts recorded four or five times this number.

The dispatches to the New York *Tribune* chronicle the event:

To the Associated Press.

PROMONTORY SUMMIT, UTAH, *May 10*—The last rail is laid! The last spike is driven! The Pacific Railroad is completed. The point of junction is 1,086 miles west of the Missouri River, and 690 miles east of Sacramento City.

LELAND STANFORD
Central Pacific Railroad.

T. C. DURANT
SIDNEY DILLON }*Union Pacific Railroad.*
JOHN DUFF

By Telegraph to the Tribune.

WASHINGTON, *May 10*—The announcement having been made here about noon today that the driving of the spikes in the last rail which would complete the line of railroad between the Atlantic and Pacific Oceans would be communicated to all the telegraph offices in the country the instant the work was done, a large crowd gathered at the main office of the Western Union Telegraph Company here to receive the welcome news. Mr. Tinker, the Manager of the office here, placed a magnetic bell in a conspicuous place, where all present could witness the performance, and connected the same with the main line notifying the various offices throughout the country that he was ready. New Orleans, New York and Boston, instantly answered that they were ready. Soon afterwards, about 2:27 p.m., many of the offices in different parts of the country began to make all sorts of inquiries of the office at Omaha, from which point the circuit was to be started. That office replied:

"To everybody; keep quiet. When the last spike is driven at Promontory Point we will say 'Done.' Don't break the circuit, but watch for the signals of the blows of the hammers."

After some little trouble in the Chicago office, and the closing of the circuit west of Buffalo, the instrument here was adjusted, and at 2:27 p.m. Promontory Point, 2,400 miles out of Washington said to the people congregated in various telegraph offices: "Almost ready. Hats off; prayer is being offered."

A silence for the prayer ensued. At 2:40 the bell tapped again and the office at the Point said: "We have got done praying. The spike is about to be presented."

Chicago replied: "We understand. All are ready in the east."

Promontory Point: "All ready now, the spike will soon be driven. The signal will be three dots for the commencement of the blows."

For a moment the instrument was silent and then the hammer of the magnet tapped the bell, one, two, three—the signal. Another pause of a few seconds, and the lightning came flashing eastwards, vibrating over 2,400 miles between the junction of two roads and Washington, and the blows of the hammer upon the spike were delivered instantly, in telegraphic accents on the bell here. At 2:47 p.m. Promontory Point gave the signal, "DONE!" The Announcement that the continent was spanned with iron.

General Sherman and a number of other prominent officials witnessed the event at the telegraphic instrument in the War Department. The president had promised to be there but a State Delegation got hold of him and detained him until it was too late.

The reporter for James Gordon Bennett's New York *Herald* wired his telegraph editor as follows:

The scene was a grassy valley on a mountain which divides the north end of Great Salt Lake into two bays, far away from all signs of civilization except such as surround the railroad camps. A chosen party of skilled Chinese levelled the ground and laid the last few ties, and the last pair of rails were laid and spiked to all but the last tie, the spikes being driven by Mr. Nottingham, President of the Michigan Central and Lake Shore Railroad. Commissioners Sherman, Hoyne, Strawbridge and Reed, superintendents of construction, placed the polished laurel tie with silver plate, sent by California, under the rail. The ends and joints were adjusted by the respective officers of the Union Pacific, taking the right hand rail looking east and the Central Pacific the left hand. Edgar Mills, as master of ceremonies, called upon Rev. Dr. Todd of Pittsfield, to invoke the blessing of the Deity on their work. Dr. Harkness, with a few words, offered California's gift of a golden spike, which was accepted by Vice-President Durant, and by him placed in the auger hole. Mr. F. A. Trittle, in the name of Nevada, offered a silver spike with a neat sentiment. Governor Stanford accepted it and placed it. Governor Safford, of Arizona, on behalf of that territory, offered a spike of gold, silver and iron, with a short sentiment. Governor Stanford responded for the railroad over which he presided. After recounting their labors and anxieties, and expressing a wish for amity, peace and cooperation between the companies, he spoke of the great future for railroads, when freights by railroad shall be less than any other mode of carriage. General Dodge responded for the Union Pacific Railroad, and concluded by saying that they had built the pathway to India.

Edgar Mills added a few words and presented a silver sledge hammer in the name of the Pacific Union Express Company. Governor Stanford received it, and the telegraph wire having been connected with it and Vice-President Durant having arrived with the ordinary tool, the signal was given and the President of the Central and the Vice-President of the Union drove home the last spikes. At Stanford's blow the electric current through hundreds of cannon made known to the world that the great work which will revolutionize commerce was accomplished, and that courage, patience and skill had achieved what was a few years ago laughed at as the dream of enthusiasts. When the shouts of joy had subsided the telegrams to the President of the United States and to the Associated Press were read, and the ceremony concluded with three cheers for every one concerned in building the road, from the laborer who did the work to the government who furnished the means. Many congratulations and expressions of mutual respect and esteem passed between officials of roads, once rivals, now united and with common interests in building up the traffic of both coasts and developing the country through which they pass. California's interest in this day's work on Promontory Summit is only second to that of finding gold at Sutter's Mill, and the results are likely to be as stupendous in their effects on the Pacific slope and on the world at large.

The following day the first trainload of passengers disembarked from a scheduled Central Pacific through varnish, tramped past the site of the last tie and boarded a scheduled Union Pacific train for Omaha. At the same time the postal authorities were notified that the through mails from the Pacific were en route and the contract with the Butterfield Company for the transportation of the overland mails of the United States came to an automatic expiration. It had cost $1,100 per mile per annum via the Concord coaches with their shot-gun messengers aloft and henceforth would cost but $200 by the iron highroad of the rails. A day later the first invoice of tea from Japan to St. Louis started to roll east, passing a few miles west of Promontory one of the last of all the caravans of covered wagons bound for California. The age of steam had been realized and its mightiest kingdom was the West.

During the period of financing and constructing the Central and later, during the first four decades of its operation, the Southern Pacific was probably subjected to more abuse and denunciation than any other financial undertaking in the history of the United States. Success and achievement, then as now, proved the most effective irritants to malice, jealousy, frustration and incompetence, indeed all the futile and thwarted qualities of second rate men customarily known as "social consciousness" and "humanitarianism." To third chop newspaper paragraphers, to ward heelers with an eye on the governorship and to novelists with a hanker to have their fiction read elsewhere than below stairs the Southern Pacific quite inadvertently lent its services.

It is not without its irony that, along with having brought the state of California into economic being and, almost single-handed, having made possible the exploitation of its fabulous resources, the Southern Pacific must also accept responsibility for the rise to notoriety of the piddling demagogues and rabble-rousers who would never have been heard above the squeakings of oblivion save through their fatuous abuse of the life-giving, the all-powerful, all-creative railroad.

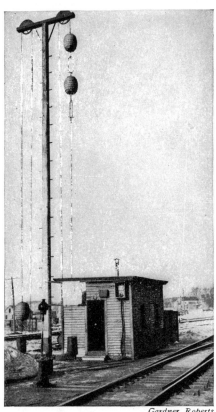

Gardner Roberts

Courtesy of the Atchison, Topeka and Santa Fe

2

SPEED

IN the middle thirties of the twentieth century the working time-table of the Atchison, Topeka and Santa Fe's Super Chief between Prowers and Caddoa, Colorado, called for a speed of 108 miles an hour over a slightly longer than ten-mile run. On this same schedule the Super Chief made the 2,228-mile run across the continent from Chicago to Los Angeles at an average of 56 miles an hour.

In the earliest days of New England railroading a century before the Super Chief speeds were less precisely clocked, but it was the discovery that the Boston and Maine would bring Lowell and Haverhill only an hour and a half from Boston compared to the two days required by way of the Middlesex Canal that finally convinced the Great and General Court of Massachusetts to grant the road a charter, and it was over the Boston and Maine's Western Division, approximately a decade later, that the world's first mile-a-minute run was established. A recent check-list of scheduled daily mile-a-minute runs in the United States added up to several hundred, many of them non-stop distance runs between 120 and 180 miles long, but in 1848 no man had yet traveled a mile in sixty seconds, and there were universal doubts expressed as to the probability of his doing it. Only fifty years before, President Washington had been advised by leading physicians that a stage-coach speed of fifteen miles an hour would invariably result in the death of any one attempting it by causing all the blood in the body to run to the head, and in 1848 a mile a minute seemed obviously against God even if it could be contrived by human ingenuity and daring. Which, of course, it couldn't.

The Boston and Maine had recently come into possession of a new ten-ton, 35-horse-power locomotive built to its order in England and shortly to be put into regular service hauling goods and passengers from the rich farmlands of New England. Long before the days of high-pressure railroad publicity men, Charles Minot, general superintendent of the road, was well aware of the uses of promotion and set about bringing the Antelope to the attention of potential shippers and passengers in a manner that would have done him credit in a much later time. Taking into his confidence his most trusted locomotive-driver named Pemberton, who had had ten years of experience, which was about all a man could possibly claim in 1848, Minot planned a *coup* which should knock the spots off any railroad publicity yet achieved by rival and less daring roads. It was advertised that a train drawn by the Antelope would attempt to make the distance of 26 miles between Boston and Lawrence in the unheard-of time of 26 minutes. Newspapers were invited to send representatives to cover the epic event, and on the morning of the great run the roofs of Haymarket Square, where the B. & M. station was then located, were black with observers intent on seeing all they could from the safest possible distance. Every switch had been spiked down, every crossing on the line was guarded by railroad police and local constables.

Under a Pain's fireworks display of wood smoke and blazing cinders representing almost half the contents of the fire-box, the Antelope got under way. There was as yet no provision for securing the cylinder cocks from the driver's seat, and the fireman, after the train had gone a little distance to get up momentum, dropped off and ran alongside to close them, regaining the deck more or less winded as the locomotive gained speed. Pemberton, Superintendent Minot and his fireman were all engaged in tossing fat pine knots into the fire-box as the train passed through Somerville. By the time they reached Malden the reporters in the wooden coach behind had commended themselves to God and were lying face down on the floor where the chances of survival seemed better, if not actually bright, when they went into the ditch. The man from the *Advertiser,* greatly daring, had ventured to look out the window a way back and, in the cloud of dust, soot and poultry feathers which rose astonishingly in their rear, had seen the strap iron rails curling up in snakeheads amidst the cadavers of ducks and chickens from farms adjacent to the right of way.

South Reading, Reading, Wilmington Junction and Ballardvale were lined with spectators standing in the meadows or safely removed to points of vantage in trees and haystacks. The Antelope unquestionably was making 60, and her bright red paint was observed to be blistering in numerous places. Just before they reached Andover, Superintendent Minot detected the odor of hot metal indicating that the steam-chest was becoming dangerously hot, and the fireman, heroic perforce, had to climb out on the footboard and souse the running parts with liquid paraffin. On the verge of shaking itself to pieces in the manner of the celebrated one-horse shay, the Antelope drew into Lawrence in 26 minutes to the split second by the hands of Superintendent Minot's Tobins-built "Rail Road Time Keeper," and the reporters were assisted from the coach by a cheering populace. It was all of an hour, the greater part of it spent in the nearby Merrimac Tavern, before the news hawks were themselves again and telling everybody how composed they had been, quite indifferent indeed to the perils of the journey. The road-bed wasn't in really good repair for a week, but the first mile-a-minute run of history won a great deal of fame and prestige for the B. & M.

Once established, mile-a-minute speeds became entirely unremarkable in standard railroad operation throughout the middle of last century although until the advent of 120-mile-an-hour streamliners the phrase remained in the American vocabulary as a racy superlative.

Speaking in general terms, high speeds were indulged only in short and occasional bursts on the working time-tables of the industry until the late eighties and early nineties, at about which time the high average of miles an hour became one of the main objectives of road operation and has been a principal concern of both freight and passenger service ever since. But it is only in comparatively recent times that freight service comparable in speed to the time-cards of *de luxe* varnish trains has been evolved by such trains as the Frisco's Flash between St. Louis and Tulsa and Oklahoma City and the Illinois Central's sensational MS-1 with its saving of an entire day between the Great Lakes and the Gulf of Mexico for freight of general classifications. Hotshot freight at stepped-up speed in the decades preceding the war was largely confined to perishable fruits, vegetables and other foodstuffs and, of course, the celebrated silk trains from the Pacific coast.

In September, 1891, Engineer Charlie Hogan of the New York Central and Hudson River Railroad, driving a series of William Buchanan–

designed eight-wheelers of the same class as No. 999 which was to make such a stir under his guidance two years later, rolled a special trainload of executives over the 436.5 miles between New York and Buffalo in 439.5 minutes, not counting out time for stops, to the amazement of all concerned. Only a hotbox at Fairport prevented the run being made in much faster time. Locomotives were changed twice—at Albany and at Syracuse—and the world was very properly impressed by the record of the performance as reported next morning in the public prints. Indeed it took up two dense columns of type on the front page of *The Sun*, and it was apparent both to the traveling public and to railroad executives that an age of high average speeds over extended runs was at hand.

There were, along the turn of the century, other speeds run which fired the public imagination and lent impetus to the Casey Jones tradition of American railroading. There was the run for more than four miles at a clocked rate of 115.2 miles an hour over the iron of the Philadelphia and Reading near Atlantic City and the fabled Plant Line record, hung up in Florida in the course of a mail-contract award race, of five miles covered in two and a half minutes, just 120 miles an hour. There was, too, the run of the Transcontinental Mail on the Union Pacific which has passed into roundhouse legend, with its hero Bill Downing and its setting along the reverse curves of the western slope of the Wasatch. Downing covered the 76 steep downhill miles from Evanston to Ogden over one of the most dangerous mountain divisions in the world in 65 minutes to win a Federal mail contract for the U.P., but the record itself cannot suggest the truly epic qualities of the run. One must know the division to appreciate it.

One of the most famous of all the fast runs of a more naïve age of railroading was that of the Death Valley Scotty Special over the Santa Fe and, because the account has not been as widely circulated as those of various other fast hauls, the Santa Fe's official contemporary chronicle of this hair-raising occasion is reprinted here at some length.

At one o'clock in the afternoon of Sunday, July 9, 1905, a special train, chartered by Mr. Walter Scott, pulled out of La Grande Station of the Santa Fe System, at Los Angeles. The train consisted of engine number 442, baggage car 210, dining car 1407, and the standard Pullman car Muskegon, the three cars weighing exactly 170 tons. This was the train which came to be known as the Death Valley Coyote and the Scott Special.

At 11:54 on the forenoon of July 11th, it came to a stop in the Dearborn Street Station, Chicago, having made the run of 2,265 miles in 44 hours and 54 minutes. The record stands unparalleled in railroad history.

The best previous run between these points had been made by the Lowe Special over the same road in August, 1903, which covered the distance in 52 hours and 49 minutes. The latter train, however, ran westbound and carried only a baggage and Pullman car. The best record on the eastbound run was made by the Peacock Special in March, 1900, Los Angeles to Chicago, over the Santa Fe, in 57 hours and 56 minutes, carrying a Pullman sleeping-car and a buffet-smoking car.

The story of this latest epoch-making feat of railroading has been told graphically in the public press. From edition to edition its details leaped into large type in the newspapers, were caught up and passed from lip to lip, the whole continent catching the sporting spirit of this mad dash from the Pacific to the Great Lakes.

To the general public it meant, in the main, the freak of a speed-mad miner; to railroad men the run of the Coyote was a matter of much more engrossing interest. Many of them did not sleep while the train was on the road. It was not the picturesque, even grotesque, spectacle of a blue-shirted dare-devil shaking hands with death, delirious with delight in danger, that kept them tense. It was the growing joy of the accomplished fact, the steady conquering of the seemingly impossible, the imminent fulfillment of careful calculations— something, too, of the sobering sense of an unusual responsibility.

A few minutes before noon on Saturday, the eighth of July, a man walked into Mr. John J. Byrne's private office, in the Conservative Life Building, Los Angeles. Mr. Byrne is General Passenger Agent of the Santa Fe lines west of Albuquerque. The stranger wore a cheap serge suit, a blue woolen shirt, high-heeled vaquero boots, a cowboy hat, and a fiery red tie. He pitched the hat into one corner of the office, tossed his coat on a settee, and dropping into a chair remarked quietly: "Mister Byrne, I've been thinking some of taking a train over your road to Chicago. I want you to put me in there in forty-six hours. Kin you do it?"

General Passenger Agent Byrne whistled.

"Forty-six hours?" said he. "That's a big contract, Mr. Scott. That is eleven hours and fifty-six minutes faster than the eastbound run has ever been made. Man, do you realize that half the road is over mountain divisions?"

"I ought to," answered Scott. "I've been over the Santa Fe thirty-two times between here and Chicago. I ought to! Here's the money!" And the man in the blue shirt began to shed $1,000 bills.

"I'm willing to pay any old figure, but I want to make the TIME! Kin you do it for me, or can't you? Let's talk business!"

Mr. Byrne drew out his pencil, and as he figured he talked. The miner broke in every few minutes with a shrewd remark.

The conference lasted a long time, and in the end Mr. Byrne put the $5,500 in his safe.

The train had been bought and paid for.

"Young man," said Mr. Byrne, "the Santa Fe will put you into Chicago in forty-six hours, if steam and steel will hold together. We've got the road-bed, the equipment, and the men; don't forget that. But let me tell you that you'll be riding faster than a white man ever rode before!"

"Pardner," said Scott, simply, "I like your talk. It sounds good to me. Line 'em up all along the way and tell 'em we're coming."

An hour before the time appointed, the Coyote Special was standing in the depot. Thousands of curious sightseers were on hand to see the miner start on his wild ride for a record. As the time drew near, the crowd increased until the train sheds were packed and from every eminence faces looked down.

A big engine slowly backed up and wheezed into place at the head of the train. It was No. 442 in charge of Engineer John Finlay. A big automobile dashed up to the entrance of the station and Walter Scott alighted. He had to fight his way through the crowd to get to the train. Entering the cab, he shook hands with the engineer, greeted the fireman, and, urged by the crowd, made a short speech from the tender.

In the meantime the party who were to accompany him had boarded the train. Mrs. Scott, a comely young woman, altogether without nerves, awaited her husband in the Pullman. C. E. Van Loan, the newspaper representative who was to write the story of the run, busied himself with his typewriter, and the writer hereof completed the quartette.

At last the clock pointed to the hour, old No. 442 gave a warning toot, visitors scrambled off the train, Conductor George Simpson raised a long forefinger and the Coyote began to move. A great cheer went up from the spectators, Scott waved his slouch hat in response and inside of fifteen seconds the Coyote disappeared from sight.

The passage through the city was a fleeting ovation, crowds lining every side street to see the train dash along. The little towns outside Los Angeles flitted by like shadows, the cheers of the crowds shrilling an instant and then dropping away from the tail of the racing train.

Thirty-five miles out of Los Angeles, the jar of the air brakes told that something was wrong. The big engine was slowing down and high on the flank of the mountain of steel, a fireman was clinging.

"Too bad!" said Conductor Simpson. "The tank box has gone hot on us! The fireman's playing the hose on it."

But the trouble was immediately rectified and then the train began to whiz in earnest. John Finlay meant to make up that lost time. And he did. One hour and fifteen minutes had been the railroad schedule to San Bernardino. The Coyote cut ten minutes off this time. Here a helper engine was picked up and in a few minutes the engine-drivers were attacking the heavy grade of the Cajon Pass. Up near Summit, at the crest of the hill, we saw the first bit of what to the amateur railroaders of the party seemed almost miraculous railroading. A mile before we reached Summit the helper engine was un-coupled on the fly and, while the speed of the train never slackened for an instant, the light engine dashed ahead, ran onto a siding, the switch was thrown back and the oncoming special whirled over the crest of the hill.

Here it was a different story. We were on our first descending grade. The problem now was not how fast we could run, but how fast we dared run. So we shot down toward Barstow at a mile a minute, turning and twisting in and out, Engineer Finlay's hand always on the air-brake. When we made the mile between mile-posts 44 and 43 in 39 seconds, or at the rate of 96 miles an hour, we began to feel that the great race was fairly on.

We whistled into Barstow 26 minutes ahead of the killing schedule which had been laid out for us. That 26 minutes was the gift of Engineer Finlay and his crew, and anyone looking for good railroading may rely on them to repeat it as often as the call comes in.

At Barstow we changed engines for the race across the desert. It was a warm run from Barstow to the Needles, but the Coyote took it on the fly, causing the lizards hastily to hunt their holes and making the cacti by the roadside look like a hedge fence.

At 7:13 the Colorado River shimmered in the distance; at 7:17 the Coyote came to a standstill at the head of the Needles yard. In exactly eighty seconds the train was moving again, a fresh engine taking up the work. Thousands lined the track near the depot, but they had no more than a fleeting glimpse of the flying special and she was gone.

Twelve tortuous miles below Needles the Santa Fe crosses the Colorado River on a steel cantilever bridge—a marvel of modern engineering, flung solidly across a wide tawny stream. Engineer Jackson swung over that twisting track at 65 miles an hour and the glasses leaped in the diner. A rush of sound, a creaking of the bridge timbers, and with a dull whirl the Coyote found Arizona soil.

To quote verbatim from a dispatch to the "Kansas City Star":

"Have you ever seen the salt cellars playing ping pong with each other? It is not conducive to a healthy appetite. One gets to wondering what would happen if an engine should take the ditch going at that rate of speed. The correspondent looked over at the conductor, Tom Brayil, and it was great relief to an amateur record-breaker to note that he was still smiling. 'Jackson don't know a curve when he sees one,' called the conductor across the car. 'The whole road looks straight to him.'

"Here is the menu of the Death Valley Coyote, eaten at sixty miles an hour over a mountain division:

Caviare Sandwich a la Death Valley   Iced Consomme.
Porterhouse Steak a la Coyote, two inches thick, and a
Marvel of Tenderness.
Broiled Squab on Toast, with Strips of Bacon au Scotty.
Stuffed Tomatoes.
Iced Cream with Colored Trimmings.
Cheese.   Coffee.   Cigars.

"Now, where can you beat that, Mr. Epicure? Hats off to Chef Geyer, who will see the trip through to Chicago. Mr. Geyer has been many years in the service of Fred Harvey, and when he was slated to make this run, his wife objected seriously. She reminded Geyer of his four small children and bade him let some other man break his neck on the Coyote Special.

" 'Und I say to her,' explained Geyer, 'if dot man in der enchine can stand it to pull der train, I can stand it to ride behind him, yet.'

"Any man who can cook like that at sixty miles an hour is worthy a place in the culinary hall of fame."

Three hours of hard mountain railroading brought us to Seligman, where we picked up an hour. Division Superintendent Gibson climbed into the Pullman and his first facetious words were: "What detained you?" Jackson's daredevil run will go down in song and story as the most spectacular dash of the western section.

Then began the real fight of the trip—a war against heavy grades. Clouds of sparks whirled by the windows—the little Arizona towns winked once as the Coyote passed. It was here, they said, that we were to win or lose, for if we could make the schedule up and down the divides which separate Seligman from Albuquerque, win over the famous Glorieta Pass, and hold our own on the Raton Mountains, the record was ours beyond question.

It is impossible, recalling the events of that nerve-racking night, to pick out for special mention the names of the railroad heroes who won for their road a victory over those grim Arizona mountains.

I only know that from time to time crews of stern-visaged men succeeded one another; that engines were changed in record haste, and that Division Superintendent Gibson, heavy-jawed, laconic, and resourceful, rode the train, alert, confident and conquering. Outside the cool mountain wind swept through the stunted pines and over all twinkled the clear stars of the great Southwest.

There was no sleep on board the Coyote that night. In far-off cities tireless presses were reeling off the story of the flying Coyote, and on board the train "Van" hammered away at his staggering typewriter, clicking off the tale of the run which now belongs to railroad history.

18 Hours to Chicago

THE FASTEST LONG DISTANCE TRAIN IN THE WORLD.

JUNE 11, 1905

"THE PENNSYLVANIA SPECIAL"

WILL BE PLACED IN SERVICE ON THE

PENNSYLVANIA RAILROAD

BETWEEN

NEW YORK AND CHICAGO

ON THE FOLLOWING SCHEDULE DAILY:

Lv. New York (W. 23d St.)	...3.55 P. M.	Lv. Chicago	...2.45 P. M.
" " (Desb. and Cort. Sts.)	...4.00 "	Ar. New York	...9.45 A. M.
" Brooklyn	...3.45 "	" Brooklyn	...9.50 "
Ar. Chicago	...8.55 A. M.		

PULLMAN PARLOR SMOKING CAR, DRAWING-ROOM SLEEPING CARS, DINING CAR, AND COMPARTMENT OBSERVATION CAR

A BUSINESS DAY IN EITHER CITY

W. W. ATTERBURY,	J. R. WOOD,	GEO. W. BOYD,
General Manager.	Passenger Traffic Manager.	General Passenger Agent.

Courtesy of Railroad Magazine

Competition between the Pennsylvania and New York Central Railroads has always been a stern and unrelenting matter. The day the Central put into operation the Twentieth Century Limited in 1902 the Pennsylvania inaugurated its Broadway Limited's predecessor known as the Pennsylvania Special on the New York–Chicago run. In June, 1905, the running time of the Century was reduced to 18 hours and the Pennsy immediately met this gesture by placing their competing train on a similar carding as is shown by this poster. From that day to this the two roads have run closely competing trains on the Chicago and St. Louis runs and, in 1938, when the streamlined Century was put in service, the Pennsylvania synchronously reduced its running time to meet the new 16-hour schedule and started operation of a new and magnificently appointed Broadway Limited.

It was not until the first switch at the outer edge of the Albuquerque yards clattered beneath the flying wheels that Superintendent Gibson smiled.

"I've brought you over the Albuquerque Division 34 minutes faster than any train went over it before," said he, as he bade us good-by. He had beaten the time of the Lowe Special by 34 minutes; he expected to beat it by 30.

The two Indian villages between Albuquerque and Lamy have never seen a train dropped down a hill at such a rate of speed. Engineer Ed Sears was

Courtesy of the New York Central

THE WONDER AND GLORY OF THE NINETIES

When, on September 14, 1891, Engineer Charles Hogan of the New York Central and Hudson River Railroad drove a special, carrying road executives and newspapermen from New York to East Buffalo at an average speed of 61.44 miles an hour, allowing for stops, frock-coated business men stopped their hansoms in Fifth Avenue to buy the extras telling of the fastest long-distance haul ever made on a railroad. *The Sun* devoted three front page columns to the event and Mr. Hogan never expected to get so much flattering attention again. In May, 1893, however, at the throttle of Engine 999, he drove the Empire State Express between Syracuse and Buffalo over a measured mile at a speed of 112.5 miles an hour and the whole world gasped and there were those who wouldn't believe a word of it. Gentlemen in the Holland House bar shook their heads, incredulous, when the ticker brought the news and when next year, No. 999 was placed on view at the Columbian Exposition, a guide-book to the fair remarked that "for this locomotive such impossible rates of speed have been claimed as a mile in 32 seconds." Since that time faster runs have become commonplace but the luster of the fame of Engineer Hogan and No. 999 is secure forever as part of the American legend. The photograph was taken at the Poughkeepsie track pans.

ERIE PASTORAL

A decade after Uncle Dan'l Drew, Gould, Jim Fisk and other post-bellum high-binders of Wall Street had had their way with the Erie, this early eighties action photograph was taken of a passenger local in upper New York. Its white smoke exhaust blends with the cumulus cloud rising over the background hillside to form a spectacular souvenir of a vanished era of railroading.

"THE SPARKLING NOISE OF THEIR RIDING IS EVER IN OUR EARS"

Into the Puerto del Cajon rolls the Atchison, Topeka and Santa Fe's The Chief on the 83-mile run between San Bernardino and Barstow. The summit of the Cajon is 3,800 feet above sea-level and it requires two of the Santa Fe's most powerful locomotives, a Mountain and a Northern, to haul her eleven light-weight steel cars of air-flow design up to Summit. From Summit through Lugo and Hesperia to Victorville, where the helper engine is dropped, is an easy roll and from there across the broad uplands of the San Bernardino Mountains to Barstow The Chief makes time on its fast transcontinental schedule.

THE 400

The Chicago and North Western's 400 was the first of the modern steam-drawn trains of conventional steel construction to challenge the then growing hold of light-weight streamlined Diesel-electric trains on the popular imagination. The 409-mile run between Chicago and St. Paul was carded for 390 minutes. A team of high speed heavy Pacifics was rebuilt with every improvement known to the North Western's executives: 79-inch drivers, cross-counterbalanced to assure smooth action, oil fuel installation, new main driving axles, crank-pins and piston-rods, superheater units and high-speed piston valves of new design. Passenger accommodations were modernized throughout and luxuriously decorated and a wide campaign of exploitation and publicization was undertaken. Within a few months the 400 was the most talked-of train in the land and from that day to this it has been one of the crack successful flyers of America. Rolling into the main at high speed, the 400 is shown pulling out of the North Western Station in Chicago at three o'clock of a spring afternoon.

THE SOUTHERN PACIFIC'S LARK

Train No. 76 is the night sleeper-train between San Francisco and Los Angeles over the Coast Route of the Espee. It is the sleeping accommodation counterpart of the streamlined Daylight and companion train to the Coaster, No. 69, the likeness of which illustrates the jacket of this book.

WINGED MESSENGER OF THE CENTRAL

Henry Dreyfuss, the industrial designer, planned the Mercury for the New York Central Lines and more than two years after it had been put into operation crowds gathered along the line on its Cleveland-Detroit run to watch it pass and at certain grade crossings special police were stationed to warn motorists of its deceptive speed. Streamlining, tight locked couplings, aluminum-finished exteriors and extreme spaciousness of passenger quarters are the distinctive features of the Central's first departure from more conventional train design. It averages better than a mile a minute on its run and hits 90 in spots, and its average gross revenue since its inauguration has been about $3.50 a mile. Two Class K-5 Pacifics were rebuilt and shrouded to haul the Mercury.

WHEELING THE READING'S VARNISH

Hauled by a light Pacific, No. 178, its simplicity of design as well as the flanged stack lending it a somewhat English appearance, the Reading's Seven O'Klocker, a crack express on the Philadelphia–New York run, hits 80 on the slight down-grade just west of Plainfield, New Jersey. On this locomotive, as is a more usual practice in England than in the United States, all possible pumps, lubricators and pipe-lines are concealed under the boiler-housing.

''ON THE DELAWARE LACKAWAN'''

The Delaware, Lackawanna and Western's Super-Pocono (4-8-4), No. 1602, heads east, over a freshly ballasted road-bed, out of Buffalo passing Forks, New York, with 110 cars of mixed freight in train. At Buffalo the Lackawanna meets the Nickel Plate and the two interchange both freight and passengers for the east and west at this point.

THE EMPIRE BUILDER

The famed transcontinental limited of the Great Northern, hauled by a mighty 4-8-4, eastbound on the West Coast–St. Paul–Minneapolis run, halts at Minot, North Dakota, for mails, passengers, ice, water and fuel. From Chicago to St. Paul the Empire Builder runs over the iron of the Burlington and on its long haul it features every convenience known to modern rail travel: sunroom, observation-lounge, buffet and soda-fountain, barber shop and shower-baths, valet and maid service and radio reception.

SPEED AND THE UNION PACIFIC

Photographed by Gerald M. Best, one of the foremost of railroad and locomotive cameramen of his generation, this Union Pacific special, run out of Los Angeles for a fraternal convention, represents almost the ideal action picture. Shot with a wide angle lens to insure including the entire length of the train, it catches a full, low smoke exhaust and yet stops the movement of drivers and rod assembly completely. At her smoke box the U.P. 4-8-2 flies the white markers of a special.

LAYING OVER ON THE CURVE

Hitting 80 miles an hour on a reverse curve at Weston Park Siding, Massachusetts, the Boston section of the New York Central's Southwestern Limited, Train No. 11 over the Boston and Albany, westbound for St. Louis, furnishes a dramatic example of speed photography by H. W. Pontin. The Southwestern, the long run speed-schedule of which is second only to that of the Twentieth Century Limited on the Central's train roster, connects the Atlantic seacoast with St. Louis in direct competition with the Pennsylvania's The American. Here she is hauled by the B.&A.'s Hudson, No. 619.

LIFTING TO THE HILLS

The Atchison, Topeka and Santa Fe's Grand Canyon Limited heads up into the California foot-hills on the run between San Bernardino and Barstow. A crack train on the Chicago–Los Angeles run, the Grand Canyon Limited also runs a tourist sleeper for the accommodation of passengers of more modest means.

THE PENNSY'S NEW YORKER

With fourteen cars of mail and baggage and hauled by one of the Pennsylvania's characteristic K-4s Class Pacifics, the New Yorker, one of the road's numerous fleet of Chicago–New York daily trains, picks up speed as it starts the eastbound run passing through South Chicago, Illinois. Often the New Yorker carries such a heavy load of mails and express as to run double-headed to Harrisburg where electrification commences.

THE ESPEE'S NO. 2

The Apache, which becomes Train No. 12 over the leased iron of the Rock Island as it runs into Chicago, is shown here heading east and making approximately 50 miles an hour on a misty California morning between Alhambra and Palm Springs.

Lucius Bee

MODERNITY ALONG THE ALTON

To compete with such trains as the Illinois Central's Green Diamond, the Banner Blue of the Wabash and the Chicago and Eastern Illinois' St. Louis Zipper on the daylight run between St. Louis and Chicago, the Alton (Baltimore and Ohio) a few years ago installed the Abraham Lincoln, Trains No. 2 and No. 3, on a daily roundtrip schedule between these two important midwestern cities. Diesel-powered but showing little trace of what generally passes for "streamlining," the Abraham Lincoln noses its way out of the St. Louis terminal into the morning sunshine on its northbound run.

POISED FOR THE CHICAGO RUN

The Green Diamond, speedy and luxurious daylight flyer with Diesel power of the Illinois Central Railroad, snakes out of the St. Louis terminal and heads for the Merchants' Bridge across the Mississippi. Equipped with a chair-car, a chair-buffet and a diner-lounge for parlor passengers, the Green Diamond is articulated, streamlined and air-conditioned throughout.

Lucius Be

Lucius Beebe

THE NEW ENGLAND STATES

The Boston and Albany–New York Central's crack highliner out of Boston for the West, No. 27, The New England States, rolls inland over the main iron at Palmer, Massachusetts. An all-Pullman limited, replacing the now discontinued Boston section of the Century, it is complete with all-room sleepers, lounges, club-car, diner and the brass-railed observation Pullman of tradition, and is powered by one of the B.&A.'s heavy Hudsons, whose square sand dome is one of the characteristics of this series of locomotives.

Lucius Beebe

ONCE THE OLD COLONY RAN HERE

Where once the iron of the famed Old Colony Railroad ran out of Boston, this New York, New Haven and Hartford streamlined heavy-duty Hudson of the "Shoreliner" class steams out of the yards ahead of the Gilt Edge Limited. These locomotives are classed as I-5s and are designed to handle 16-car trains on the Boston–New York run on the road's fastest schedules. Designed jointly by New Haven and Baldwin engineers, they rank in sleek beauty with the power of the Espee's Daylight and the classic series of Chicago and North Western's stream-lined steamers. The series numbers run from 1400 to 1409.

ON THE MILWAUKEE

With twelve cars of mail, express and passengers behind it, the Chicago, Milwaukee, St. Paul and Pacific's Day Express No. 6410, a heavy 4-6-4, starts west out of Chicago on the Minneapolis–St. Paul run. The Day Express is one of the Milwaukee trains supplementing the service of the road's crack Hiawatha, the equipment of which includes luxury coaches, drawing-room parlor-cars, a 48-seat restaurant-car and the famed Tip Top Tap Car.

ALONG THE ROUTE OF THE ANTELOPE

Over the Western Division of the Boston and Maine, where, ninety years before, Charlie Minot wheeled the Antelope for the first mile-a-minute run on record, the Flying Yankee, Budd-built, streamlined Diesel local, clicks off 730 miles a day on the Boston–Portland–Bangor run over the rails of the Boston and Maine and Maine Central. It is shown at speed, Wakefield, Massachusetts.

GRAND CANYON LIMITED

The Santa Fe's famous passenger train on the Pacific Coast–Chicago run, complete with maids, valets, barber shops, baths, restaurant- and compartment-cars and all the equipment of standard Pullman luxury, heads east across the meadows of San Bernardino, gaining momentum for the climb into the Cajon Pass. Locomotive No. 3738 is a Baldwin-built 4-8-2 with 69-inch drivers and a tractive force of 56,800 pounds. No. 3755 is a 4-8-4 with 73-inch drivers and a tractive force of 69,150 pounds and here they are rolling their varnish into the hills with everything wide open and valves popping.

Lucius Beebe

ROCKETS

Built by Budd and powered with 1,200 horse-power Diesel-electric engines, the Rock Island's six Rocket trains cover a wide variety of runs over that system's 8,000 miles of rails. One of the four-car Rockets here shown is on the Fort Worth–Houston–Dallas run. Others link Peoria and Des Moines and Chicago, Minneapolis and Kansas City, and Kansas City and Denver.

SPEED IN THE EIGHTIES

Among the earliest known action photographs of trains and antedated, so far as is commonly known, only by the New Haven action photographs taken in '82 for *Scientific American* and reproduced elsewhere in this volume, this shot shows the Southern Pacific's eight-wheeler, No. 73, stepping bravely along with a string of varnish at Oak Grove, now Burlingame, California, in 1884.

Courtesy of the Southern Pacific

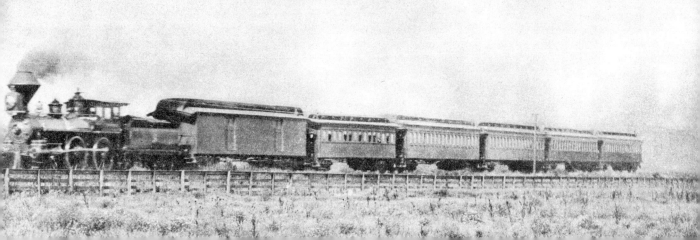

at the throttle and every inch of the track is well known to this big engineer. A helper engine swung in at Lamy for the climb to the top of the Glorieta, one of the steepest grades on the entire run, 158 feet to the mile. Back in the Pullman, Trainmaster Jim Kurn grinned as he greeted Scott.

"Here's where you get a touch of real mountain railroading," said he, "and we're going to beat the schedule if we have to sidetrack that dining car. She's got another hot box."

"Sure," said Scott. "If she smokes any more, cut 'er out!"

A few minutes later the Coyote struck the Apache Canyon, a wild bit of mountain country, memorable as the scene of many an Indian fight. At the rate of 40 miles an hour the train climbed the incline; there was a few seconds delay as the helper engine dropped out and then began the "real mountain railroading."

Down the steep grade, Sears drove his engine, the white mile posts flashing by at the rate of one every minute. The whole train lurched and staggered over the reverse curves, the typewriter carriage banged from side to side and the passengers, looking at each other, smiled. It seemed that the train must leave the track as it took those great curves and from the diner came a negro, blanched almost white. "Ah's seen a lot ob railroadin', fus an' las'," said he, "but runnin' lak dis is plumb ridiculous! Jess plumb ridiculous!" It was impossible to stand up in the leaping, swaying Pullman. One man tried it; his shoulder went through the window. After that we were all content to sit still and hang on. Only Jim Kurn was calm. He knew Sears' reputation for careful running, but it seems to me the engineer crowded the limit hard that morning. None of us were sorry when the train stopped at Las Vegas.

At Raton, Jim Kurn said good-by.

"You're a long way ahead of that schedule now," he said, "and it won't be our fault if the people east of here don't shoot you into Chicago on time! It's hard work fighting these mountains twenty-three hours out of every twenty-four, but show me a mountain railroad man who wants a job on a plains division! Good luck!"

Two engines took the Coyote at Raton. The time of the change was a trifle over a minute and we were off again. "Hud" Gardner is another mountain engineer who knows the game. He brought us into La Junta at 5:13, hours ahead of schedule and the worst part of the journey behind us.

East of La Junta lies the Santa Fe "rack track." It is here that trains are supposed to make time. With a straight track, the Kansas plains lying level as a floor and a good roadbed underneath, the Coyote took up the second part of the journey.

With Engineers Lesher, Simmons, Norton, and Halsey alternating in the cab, all the way from La Junta to Newton, the new and mighty balanced-compounds whizzed down the Arkansas Valley. "Scotty" rode the engine into Dodge, with the telegraph poles looking like a fine-tooth comb. It was from Dodge he wired President Roosevelt:

"An American cowboy is coming east on a special train faster than any cowpuncher ever rode before; how much shall I break transcontinental record?"

All that Monday night the miles flew from under the whirring wheels; in places at the rate of 85 and 90 miles an hour; the average for 300 miles being a mile every 50 seconds. The great Kipling once wrote the story of a record-breaking run East over this same road. It is a part of his "Captains Courageous." It was fiction, but it reads like fact. That is because Kipling wrote it. On almost every point covered in his narrative of the fictitious run I can say he tells the truth. He says, however, that "the ties ripple and surge away behind the flying train," and for once he is wrong. Given a reasonably straight piece of roadbed, and the faster the train goes the smoother it goes. And the ties do not ripple and surge away behind it. The roadbed just skips away, as the paper slips away from the roller of a big newspaper press. That was the way it slipped from under the wheels of the flying Scott Special.

Josiah Gossard, who has been an engineer on the Santa Fe for twenty-three years, took the train from Emporia to Argentine in the quickest time ever made between those two points—124 miles in 130 minutes, notwithstanding four slow orders and several grade crossings. Gossard has a medal, recently presented by the Shriners, for making up one and a half hours of lost time on their special, Newton to Kansas City.

It was nearly eight o'clock Tuesday morning when the Coyote crossed the Mississippi. The end was almost in sight now.

We had taken on another engineer at Ft. Madison shops just on the western edge of Illinois. He was a German named Losee. As a fine finisher in the stretch you will look a long time for his equal. Stolid, modest, destitute of nerves, he is the direct antithesis of the dare-devil engineer of fiction.

With Losee at the throttle and a straightaway stretch to the wire the Coyote cut loose for the run home across the State of Illinois. They knew all about "Scotty" and his private train in Illinois. And so they made a holiday of that July morning, and every little hamlet along the line from Shopton to Chicago turned out to cheer the Coyote on to the goal.

It was one ovation all through Illinois. And Losee was earning every bit of it. The special had made some splendid miles in Colorado and Kansas. She was to outdo them all in Illinois. Losee ran engine No. 510 from Ft. Madison to Chillicothe, 105 miles, in 101 minutes, changing at the latter point to clear track into Chicago, with every switch spiked and the entire operating department standing on its toes "rooting."

"Scotty" rode a part of the distance on the engine with Losee, and helped the fireman feed coal into the furnace.

From the little hamlet of Cameron to the still smaller one of Surrey is 2.8 miles. "She" made it in one minute and thirty-five seconds, at the rate of 106 miles an hour. The world's record before had been held by the Pennsylvania road, which covered the 2.5 miles between Landover and Anacosta in 102-miles-an-hour time. That was in August, 1895.

We lost five minutes at Chillicothe, and four more at South Joliet. Nevertheless we made the run of 239 miles from Shopton to the Dearborn Street station in Chicago in 239 minutes.

The record-breaking run was ended!

The most recent and comprehensive survey of high-speed passenger averages in the United States lists no fewer than 781 runs of better than a mile a minute on scheduled trains aggregating 46,242 miles. Of these, 717 are on daily schedules, the remainder on weekly or semi-weekly trains. A vast preponderance of these 60 mile-an-hour or better runs are accomplished by standard steam locomotives varying from the most modern designs to engines twenty-odd years in service. All the non-stop runs of more than 180 miles, however, and a substantial number of those between 150 and 180 miles, are recorded as the performances of Diesel-powered trains. As might well be imagined, the great transcontinental trains, such as the Super Chief, Denver Zephyr, City of San Francisco and City of Los Angeles, achieve most of the high-speed long-run records.

The two ranking railroads, so far as speedy daily mileage is concerned, are the Pennsylvania and New York Central with daily mile-a-minute runs of 11,500 and 8,100 miles respectively, followed by the Burlington and the Atchison, Topeka and Santa Fe, whose Diesel-powered Super Chief accounts for no less than seven of the non-stop runs of more than 180 miles accomplished at a better than 60 mile-an-hour average. By every standard, the fastest train in the land in the late thirties is the Chicago and North Western–Union Pacific Diesel-electric City of Denver on the Chicago-Denver assignment. On the eastbound run where this streamlined, super-luxury flyer enjoys a favorable grade of a full mile coming down the Colorado hillslopes, it covers the 1,048-mile overnight trip in 15 hours and 38 minutes at a slightly better average for the entire span of a third of the continent than 67 miles an hour.

TEN RECORD RUNS

FIRST MILE-A-MINUTE RUN: Locomotive Antelope, Boston to Lawrence, Massachusetts, 26 miles in 26 minutes, 1848

FIRST HUNDRED-MILES-AN-HOUR RUN: Empire State Express, between Syracuse and Buffalo, New York, a measured mile at 112.5 miles an hour, May 10, 1893

FASTEST RECORDED RUN IN HISTORY: Pennsylvania Special at Elida, Ohio, three miles at 127.2 miles an hour, June 12, 1905

SECOND FASTEST RECORDED RUN: Florida Mail, between Fleming and Jacksonville, Florida, 5 miles at 120 miles an hour, March, 1901

FASTEST CARDED START-TO-STOP RUN: City of Denver, Grand Island to Columbus, Nebraska, 62 miles at 81.3 miles an hour

FASTEST CARDED RUN OVER 2,000 MILES: City of Los Angeles, Chicago to Los Angeles, 2,299 miles at an average of 58 miles an hour

FASTEST CARDED RUN OVER 1,000 MILES: City of Denver, Denver to Chicago, 1,048 miles at an average of 67 miles an hour

FASTEST CARDED NON-STOP RUN BY STEAM: Twentieth Century Limited, Elkhart, Indiana, to Toledo, Ohio, 133 miles at an average of 75 miles an hour

FASTEST SPECIAL RUN OVER 1,000 MILES: Denver Zephyr, Chicago to Denver, 1,017 miles at an average of 83.3 miles an hour, October 23, 1936

FASTEST CARDED NON-STOP RUN OVER 100 MILES: Super Chief, La Junta, Colorado, to Dodge City, Kansas, 202 miles at an average of 78.3 miles an hour

Lucius Beebe

Lucius Beebe

3   *POWER*

IT is improbable that the steam locomotive will ever again exercise the peculiarly engaging fascination that it had for the generations that knew it in its youth. From the time of the emergence from the eccentric variations of design of its predecessors of the high-wheel American-type engine, a gleaming miracle of blue steel, brass and lacquer. through the age of its perfection at the hands of Mason and Fairbanks and, later, William Buchanan, down to the time that No. 999 reeled off the miles of that most epic of all runs, was the golden era of American railroading. Beyond the 4-4-0 there lay sophistication and the weariness of too much knowledge. The end of the Augustan Age of trains may be said to have come with the Mikado.

But since it was neither the charm of their locomotives for their contemporaries nor the wistfulness they might inspire in posterity that motivated Hinkley or McKay and Aldus or Rogers in the construction of their motive power, although the locomotive builders of last century had a consciousness of artistry that has disappeared along with crimson boiler-trim and teakwood cabs, but rather the evolution of practicable machinery, it is only suitable to view the motive power of the immediate present from the same utilitarian viewpoint. And the sleek Mountain-types and Hudsons which to-day roll into the main from the shops of Baldwin and Alco and Lima are not without their esthetic appeal to the eye cultivated to their appraisal.

Perhaps the most effective comprehension of the steam locomotive derives from viewing it as one of the simplest machines ever devised. For all its bulk and impressiveness, it uses only a few moving parts, and its essential mechanism is transparent and obvious. Quite appropriately, both its faults and virtues lie in this lack of complexity. Because it is so simple, it is theoretically very wasteful, converting approximately only a fifteenth part of the power compressed in its fuel into hauling ability. Because it is so simple, however, it is comparatively cheap to build and keep in repair, is versatile and dependable in performance.

89

Moreover, theoretical efficiency and practical economy are not necessarily identical; any society obviously must value its machines by the amount of man-power they will displace when all expenses are considered. An engine running on free air would be impractical if it needed an army of attendants to keep going; an extremely complicated perpetual motion machine probably couldn't compete with an ox cart. The very evidence, moreover, of the steam locomotive's inefficiency—the hiss of escaping steam, the drum-roll of the exhaust, the smoke that whips from the stack, the hot breath of the fire-box—is what endows it with its magnificent personality. By a happy but not altogether illogical chance, the steam locomotive may be described as a combination of beauty, simplicity and utility. It would be difficult, at any rate, to think of another man-made device in which these qualifications complement one another so neatly. The essentials of a steam locomotive are a boiler, a coupled arrangement of pistons and connecting-rods, and wheels. The boiler generates the steam; the steam pushes the pistons and rods back and forth, and the rods turn the wheels. And just as the art of designing engines consists largely in deciding on the measurements of these essentials, so the characteristics of the machines depend largely upon the ratios between them.

Since steam is what makes it go, the engine's absolute power is dependent upon the capacity of the boiler; and two locomotives with precisely the same boiler capacity, no matter how different they are in every other way, develop exactly the same power. This does not necessarily mean that the two engines can pull the same train, or that they can run equally fast with a load. The specific type of work a locomotive can do best depends upon the ratio of its boiler measurements to those of its cylinders and wheels. If constructed with big cylinders, it obviously can start a greater load than with small cylinders, and if built with both big cylinders and relatively small wheels, it can start an even greater load. But this pair of large pistons propelling this heavy load will soon be traveling back and forth so rapidly that it exhausts the steam as fast as the boiler can produce it. When that occurs, the engine has reached the speed limit for the load it is pulling.

On the other hand, if the same size engine is built with small cylinders, they can move back and forth considerably more swiftly before they exhaust the capacity of the boiler. When they are connected to large driving-wheels that is even more true—not entirely because the wheels are large, but because large driving-wheels don't permit it to start such a heavy load in the first place. An engine with small driving-wheels can run as swiftly as any other provided the size of its train is limited to what it could haul if it had large wheels; the most important function of large driving-wheels is to keep the pistons and rods from moving so fast they pound themselves to pieces.

All of which reduces itself to the simple statement that the work a locomotive can do and the speed it can attain depend primarily on its ability to manufacture steam, and consequently that it must choose between using its steam to roll an enormous load comparatively slowly, or to wheel a lighter train that much more swiftly.

For the best part of a century, however, locomotive designers and builders emphasized what is known as starting tractive force, or starting pulling-power. There were a good many sound reasons for this practice. One was that high speed wasn't necessary, even if the rails in use had been smooth and heavy enough to make it feasible. Another was that the bulk of the weight of the small engines in those days was carried on the driving-wheels, and since tractive force, for best results, ought to be approximately equal to a quarter of the weight on the drivers, the ratio of tractive force to total weight (and hence to the size of the boiler) was usually relatively high.

Tractive force, which is the amount of pull exerted by an engine before the amount of power required to move the engine and tender has been deducted, is figured by dividing the total push on the cylinders (in pounds per square inch) by the diameter of the driving-wheels (in inches); and although the pressure of the steam is an important factor in the formula, there is nothing in it which appraises the ability of the boiler to keep up that pressure. If one of the New York Central Hudson-types, for instance, were fitted with a boiler half the regular size and everything else left the same, its theoretical starting tractive force would still be the same, even though its real power would be reduced by half. As a matter of fact, its actual starting tractive force would be the same.

Lucius Be

It could walk off with just as heavy a train. But before it reached 35 miles an hour, its boiler would be evaporating water as fast as it possibly could—and the engine would be traveling as swiftly as it could with that load.

Now, since the weight of an engine can't help being in direct proportion to the size of the boiler, it stands to reason that the ratio of starting tractive force to total weight affords a convenient indication of a locomotive's characteristics. That is to say, an engine weighing 300,000 pounds and exerting 40,000 pounds of tractive force can wheel its heaviest load much faster than one weighing the same but exerting 50,000 pounds of tractive force. The former, as we've already pointed out, will roll on larger wheels and probably will be equipped with smaller cylinders than the latter. And so, though these locomotives are capable of developing the same power, the power of the former is aimed at propelling lighter trains at higher speeds, and the power of the latter at dragging a heavier train at lower speed. This is precisely the difference between a freight and passenger locomotive.

We've said that engine designers and builders at one time emphasized tractive force. In the case of the freight locomotive, they grossly over-emphasized it, so closely adjusting dimensions that the total weight of the engine sometimes hardly amounted to more than four times the rated tractive force. Often the engine was "over-cylindered": had so much starting power that the wheels would be apt to spin if the power wasn't handled just so. And when it finally did get its enormous train rolling, the best it could do was 25 or 30 miles an hour, or possibly 40, where the grade was favorable. Being a steam locomotive, it could be worked above capacity. That meant (and still means) that the crew, by expert handling, could humor it along, feed the fire-box more fuel (but not too much more) than it should have had, and rattle and blast their way over the division in triumph.

The same thing held true in lesser degree for passenger locomotives. The exceptions occurred on the roads which went in for fast running, 30 to 50 years ago, and developed passenger engines with many characteristics of the best modern machines. Their ratio of weight to tractive force was sometimes seven to one; when hooked onto a train weighing two or three times as much as they did, they could travel as swiftly as anybody cared to ride. About the most striking examples that come readily to mind were the comely eight-wheelers of William Buchanan, superintendent of motive power of the New York Central and Hudson River Railroad (now New York Central), which were doing in the field of speed nearly everything that streamlined Diesel-electrics are to-day. The famous 999, which achieved 112.5 miles an hour with the Empire State Express in 1893, was one of them; and yet she is said to have been, if anything, inferior to the others. On the Lake Shore and Michigan Southern (now the New York Central between Buffalo and Chicago), eight-wheelers were also turning in remarkable records. In

1905 a special train covered the 525 miles between Chicago and Buffalo in 453 minutes, including time out for several engine changes, averaging more than 70 miles an hour when actually running. If it had continued on to New York City at its average rate, it would have made the whole trip in less than 14 hours. The Pennsylvania's regular engines, too, were handling scheduled trains at breath-taking speeds; on June 12, 1905, one of them, with the Pennsylvania Special, attained 127 miles an hour for three miles near Ada, Ohio. Contrary to general impression, fast running in those days was not made only under especially favorable conditions, with switches spiked and all other trains side-tracked and everybody hanging on for dear life; it was a commonplace occurrence for the machines which could do it.

For all that, these engines did not realize the ultimate potentialities of the steam locomotive. Their designers thought they could step-up speed indefinitely by increasing the size of the driving-wheels, but they discovered there was no substitute for steam, and the only way to make steam was to allow proportionately more space for the fire-box and more boiler surface for it to heat. The 999 herself demonstrated this truth quite effectively. Though her drivers were six inches higher than those of her sister engines, she was not so satisfactory in ordinary service, and probably could have run no faster if put to a fair test.

About the time locomotive men began to appreciate the importance of increasing heating surface other things were happening which ended the search for greater everyday speeds. Cars were steadily growing heavier, and the new steel coaches were even more heavy. Railroads began to be more "efficient," which meant that longer trains were the order of the day, and that increased engine size was promptly converted into increased starting tractive force rather than more steam at high speed. By 1910 the vogue for speed had given way to the practice of hitching the iron horse to all the cars it could haul and then adding a couple more for good measure. Pacific-type passenger engines weighing 120 tons were designed to exert a starting pull of nearly 20 tons, which meant they were expected to handle (over fairly level ground) a dozen or more 60-ton cars on schedules demanding average start-to-stop speeds of around 40 miles an hour. No matter how fast they could travel if given a chance, these engines could not wheel such heavy trains on streamlined schedules.

The decade after 1910 saw locomotives grow merely bigger and bigger. The Mikado or 2-8-2 type sometimes weighed 175 tons, and when it got too heavy the Santa Fe or 2-10-2 type followed. The 4-6-2 or Pacific-type, also gaining weight, had to be revised as a 4-8-2 or Mountain-type, while the old Atlantic or 4-4-2, a really high-speed machine, could not develop enough tractive force to be useful on swift main line trains, and yet was too fast for branch line locals, and was gradually relegated to the scrap-heap.

This was also the decade of standardization. Now that only three important American locomotive builders were left, the rest having been absorbed or gone out of business, engines resembled one another more and more, both in looks and mechanism. There was no compelling reason why they shouldn't have; with not many exceptions they were being built for more or less the same kind of work. Then came the War, during which the United States Government took over the railroads and operated them through the United States Railroad Administration. Among other things, the U.S.R.A. immediately drew up a standard design for each wheel arrangement, and all engines built during the rest of the War conformed pretty rigorously to these designs. Modifications of them were being turned out only a few years ago. Embracing all the tested motive-power ideas of their time, the U.S.R.A. designs offer particularly good examples of what American engines were like between 1910 and 1925.

Before looking at them, a word about engine types. All locomotives are classified by wheel arrangement, partly because it presents a simple, visually appreciable way of doing so, and partly because engines of a certain wheel arrangement have characteristics common to others of the same arrangement. But the latter fact is hardly more than a coincidence; a locomotive designer who thought only in terms of wheel arrangement could not get very far. Essentially, what a specific railroad wants in an engine is the ability to do a certain job within the clearance and weight limitations of its right of way, and is not essentially concerned whether the locomotive rolls on six wheels or on twelve, so long as it rolls on the fewest possible commensurate with its weight. So immediately, in addition to being circumscribed by the knowledge that he cannot build much higher than fifteen feet or much wider than ten feet, the designer is told what the total weight of the engine must not exceed, and, most important, what the weight on a single axle must not exceed. This last consideration is really what determines wheel arrangement; and it explains why a machine of a given capacity and weight may not turn out to be the same type and classification when built for two different railroad systems.

Suppose a line were in the market for passenger locomotives, and that although its bridges and track would easily support a 200-ton engine, they can't stand more than 28 tons on any one axle. It is easy to see that engine has to run on at least eight axles. Since it is generally considered conventional to equip passenger engines with a four-wheel leading truck, two of those axles are already accounted for. A moment's figuring will show that a fire-box roomy enough to generate the heat for a modern 200-ton engine would have to be carried on a four-wheel trailing truck. That would leave four driving axles (eight driving-wheels), and the engine therefore would turn out to be what the French (who somewhat more logically count only the axles) would call a 2-4-2 type, and what we (who count the wheels) call a 4-8-4 type. But for a railroad whose tracks will support a weight of 35 tons on each axle, at least one axle could be dispensed with, and the machine could very well be a Hudson or 4-6-4 type. On the other hand, for a railroad like the Russian system, where 25 tons are all an axle can carry, a 200-ton engine would need nine or possibly ten axles, resulting in an articulated 4-6-6-4 or a straight 4-12-4 type. Indeed, when the Russians recently essayed to build a freight engine weighing some 230 tons, they adopted the 4-14-4 wheel arrangement for the machine, thereby achieving a new high example of what theory can do if untempered by practical experience. By contrast, our heaviest 4-8-4 type engines weigh nearly 250 tons. While these examples conveniently omit other considerations, some of which will be discussed later, their lesson is entirely valid. Wheel arrangement tells much about engines, and is responsible for most of the differences in appearance, but in many respects it is arbitrary, and does not always indicate the real difference between them.

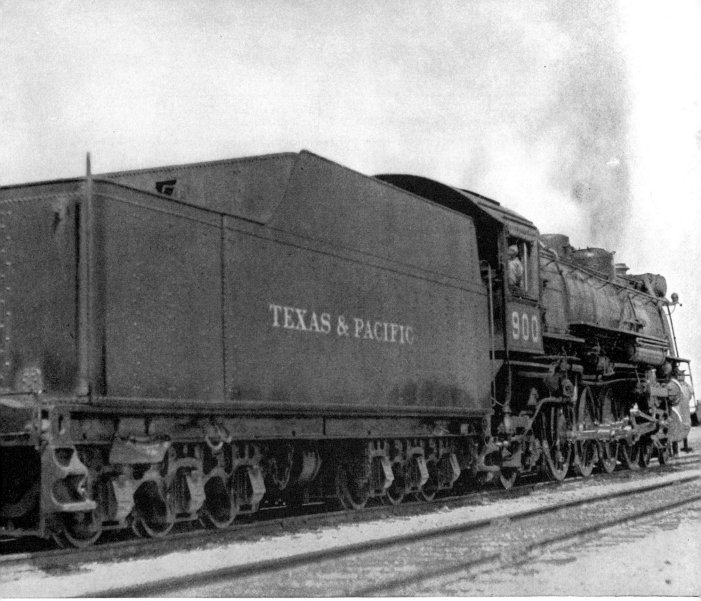

Lucius Beebe

The most important U.S.R.A. designs, for present purposes, fall into four wheel arrangements: the 4-6-2 or Pacific, the 4-8-2 or Mountain, the 2-8-2 or Mikado, and the 2-10-2 or Santa Fe types. Roughly speaking, the latter two were intended for freight and the former for passenger service, though the 4-8-2 has always been employed for both. Each type was designed in both a heavy and light model, the former being about 10 per cent more powerful and heavy than the latter.

All these U.S.R.A. engines are what a locomotive builder to-day would call very conservatively proportioned. They represented the result of nearly a hundred years' trial and error, and were nicely adapted for moving the nation's freight and transporting its passengers at that time.

Thanks to the versatility of the steam-engine the potentialities of each
type partially overlapped that of its adjacent types, and some of them
have adjusted themselves to the most modern conditions without any
trouble. The Pennsylvania's Class K-4, which wheels all its swiftest
passenger trains west of Harrisburg (including the streamlined Broadway Limited), many of them on schedules demanding average speeds of
more than 70 miles an hour, is practically the same as the U.S.R.A. heavy
Pacific-type.

But, no matter how superbly the K-4 still performs, it would be injudicious to imply that no progress had been made in steam locomotive
design since 1918; the truth is that the advances of the last fourteen
years or so are just about the most important and drastic in the history
of railroading. Stimulated first by nothing more than the desire to improve the locomotive, and later by highway competition and the Diesel-
electric engine, steam men have re-arranged the dimensions of
contemporary locomotives so that most of these U.S.R.A. engines are
obsolete, or at least would not be offered for general use to-day. Consider, for a moment, some of the characteristics of the U.S.R.A. locomotives.

The difference between the light and heavy Pacific-type is really one
of size; despite the 79-inch driving-wheels of the big engine, it no doubt
can pull its heaviest train only a little faster than that of the smaller one,
which has 73-inch driving-wheels. The reason is that it has only a little
more heating surface and no more grate area (which are indexes of
steaming capacity) for each pound of rated tractive force than the
smaller engine. Which is to say, its dimensions have been only uniformly
increased over those of the smaller one. The larger engine, it is true,
will not wear itself out so readily at high speed; when running a mile
a minute its drivers revolve only 255 times a minute, against 277 times
for the smaller wheels. But the important thing to remember about them
is that their ratio of starting tractive force to weight and boiler size is
rather low for the most modern service. When coupled to all the cars
they can start conveniently, these 4-6-2s are capable of achieving between 75 and 80 miles an hour, under ordinary conditions and without

Lucius Beebe

"UP FROM THE SOUTH AT BREAK OF DAY"

One of the night sleeping trains from Florida over the tracks of the Southern as it heads up on the Richmond, Fredericksburg and Potomac a few miles south of Alexandria. The heavy exhaust effect derives from the slight grade up which the locomotive is pulling and the sub-zero weather which prevailed at dawn when the picture was taken.

NARROW-GAGE PASTORAL

The romance of the narrow-gage railroads has always exercised a compelling hold
upon the imagination. The little pikes flourished, for the most part, in an age
when railroading was a more adventurous calling than it is to-day and the more
celebrated of them, like the Virginia and Truckee, the Denver and Rio Grande,
Colorado Central and the South Park and Pacific, had their being in the far West
or, like the Wiscasset, Waterville and Farmington and the Bridgeton and Har-
rison, in the depths of New England. There were many others: the Colorado Mid-
land and Denver, the Sandy River and Rangely Lakes, the Missouri-Southern
and the Brattleboro and Whitehall. Among the more romantic and famous narrow-gage lines and perhaps the richest of them all, the Virginia and Truckee,
which served Virginia City and Carson City in the days of the Comstock Lode,
achieved the brightest luster in the railroad legend. Close behind it comes the
Denver and Rio Grande where Fred Jukes shot this action photograph of a typical
freight along the turn of the century. In wild and often desolate settings and
breathing a pioneering fragrance, the narrow gages flowered as long as their
economic life span allowed, and to this day the ghosts of their little varnish
trains and triple-headed drags haunt the abandoned rails and switching yards of
Leadville and Mound House, Gunnison and Tonopah.

Railroad Photographs

MAIN LINE EAST

A Pennsylvania Super-Santa Fe, 2-10-2 type, No. 7697, heading out of Canton, Ohio, with 110 cars of coal bound for Harrisburg, Pennsylvania.

FORT WORTH AND DENVER CITY NO. 2-22

Chuffing out of the Fort Worth, Texas, terminal yards behind a Burlington Pacific, No. 551, this passenger and mail train will pass northwards over the iron of the Fort Worth and Denver City and the Colorado and Southern a distance of 835 miles to arrive at Denver the next morning.

Lucius Beebe

Lucius Beebe

KENNEBEC LIMITED

The Boston and Maine–Maine Central Kennebec Limited, drawn by a light Pacific, passing through Wakefield, Massachusetts, at speed.

ESPEE EXCURSION

*per left: Railroad
otographs*

Behind a heavy 4-6-0, No. 2365, the Southern Pacific's Special Bay Shore Excursion for Santa Cruz pulls out of the San Francisco yards in the early morning under a billowing cloud of oil smoke.

TWO HUNDRED TONS OF POWER

*er left:
ius Beebe*

Surging over the speed rails with the urgency of a hot cargo of fruit and stock cars, this Texas and Pacific 2-10-4 locomotive (Texas-type), representing more than 200 tons of steam and steel, is battling a slight grade over the rolling Texas country-side just south of Longview. At Texarkana, a few miles to the north, it will start over the rails of the Missouri Pacific for the long run into St. Louis.

Railroad Photographs

UNION PACIFIC

The Redball, a fast Union Pacific manifest freight, breasting the famous Sherman Hill climb, westbound, in Wyoming. No. 9000 is the first of the much exploited series of 4-12-2 three-cylinder simple Union-type locomotives, designed for utility on the western runs rather than for esthetics, but none the less a not unmajestic locomotive. This is the standard freight power on the main line between Ogden and Omaha.

WITH WHITE FLAGS FLYING

Heading for the reaches of West Texas and, eventually, El Paso, this mixed freight is rolling 50 miles an hour over the Texas and Pacific's rails behind a graceful 2-8-2, No. 803. The Texas and Pacific is the principal link between New Orleans, Shreveport, Fort Worth and the Pacific coast, the nearest parallel iron being that of the Santa Fe which approximates its route some three hundred miles to the north where it passes Amarillo in the Panhandle.

MAIN LINE LYRIC

Long before the era of light meters and panchromatic films, A. F. Bishop, a New Haven, Connecticut, photographer, started taking action photographs of trains and developing them on a wet plate a few moments after their exposure. This classic New York, New Haven and Hartford eight-wheeler, with five cars behind it and a hogger with a bowler hat, is being saluted by a smart young lady of the eighties complete with pancake hat, black mitts and parasol in a manner suggestive of the most modern advertising technique.

THE SILK EXPRESS

The great days of silk expresses are over, but the legend of swift handling of precious cargo is an integral part of the saga of railroading. The decline in the price of silk from approximately $8.00 per pound to about $1.00 between the years 1920 and the present and the consequent reduction of interest and insurance charges has ended the urgency which once attended its shipment east from the Pacific coast. The heaviest shipment of silk on record left San Francisco in December, 1921, in 21 specially designed baggage-cars of the Southern Pacific and was insured for $6,720,000. It was delivered in New York 72 hours later, much better than the fastest passenger service at that time.

Upper right: Railr Photographs

THUNDER AT BATAVIA

In order to get this stirring smoke exhaust the photographer had told the train crew in advance where he would be stationed as this giant New York Central Mallet with a 2-6-6-2 wheel arrangement pounded down the main near Batavia, New York, with a mile of company coal from the Pennsylvania mines behind.

Lower right: Railr Photographs

THE WHEELING AND LAKE ERIE'S TONNAGE

This sleek and gleaming Berkshire-type freight locomotive, on its maiden trip, is getting under way at twilight from Brewster, Ohio, for Toledo with a 110-car drag behind it. An important coal and iron road in the dense industrial region of the middle west, the Wheeling and Lake Erie has scarcely any passenger service at all but hauls thousands of tons daily of heavy merchandise in the Great Lakes area. The Berkshire 2-8-4 locomotive was first designed and built for the Boston and Albany whose iron climbs through the Berkshire Hills of western Massachusetts.

Courtesy of the Baldwin Locomotive Works

HOTSHOT EAST

This Baldwin-built, single-expansion 2-8-8-2 locomotive on the Western Pacific
is breasting a 2 per cent grade near Antelope, Nevada, with a consist of refrigerated
cars running fruit to the eastern market. At Salt Lake the Western Pacific meets
the Denver and Rio Grande Western for the haul over the Rockies to Colorado
and the trunk lines connecting with Chicago and the Atlantic seaboard.

THE OVERLAND LIMITED

The Overland Limited, whose antecedent varnish started east from Promontory the day after the Golden Spike was driven, heads into the Chicago yards. It is hauled by a powerful Hudson of airflow design christened by the classical scholar-president of the Chicago and North Western, Fred W. Sargent, The Aeolus.

SUNSET AND METEOR

The Frisco's Meteor heads into the deep southwest at Webster Grove, Missouri, behind a beautifully designed Mountain-type engine fresh and gleaming from the road's shops at Springfield.

ON THE MONTREAL–CHICAGO OVERNIGHT RUN

The Canadian Pacific Railway's Canadian, a pool train on the Montreal-Chicago run routed by way of Detroit over the Michigan Central, snapped as she pulled out of the Windsor Station, Montreal, behind a Canadian National Hudson, No. 5703, equipped with smoke-deflector and tank-type tender.

Courtesy of the Baldwin Locomotive Compa

INTERIOR BY BALDWIN

The back head of a modern freight and passenger service 4-8-4 steam locomotive
built at Philadelphia for the Denver and Rio Grande Western Railroad.

Courtesy of the General Railway Signal Company

MODERN CLASSIFICATION

The scene is the Westbound Dewitt Yard of the New York Central showing details of retarders and classification switching. In the immediate foreground are visible the retarders, controlled from the switching towers which guide freight-cars to the multiplicity of geometrically aligned tracks beyond. For contrast the insert shows an old time three-way switch and water-tower at Los Olivos, southern terminus of the Central Pacific in the sixties. Below: A train-dispatcher in the late eighties.

THIS TRAIN WAS UNIQUE

The Wheeling and Lake Erie maintained until recently but one passenger train a day, running between Cleveland and Wheeling, the vast proportion of its business being the coal haul between West Virginia and the Great Lakes region. This is it: No. 32, powered by a trim Atlantic-type locomotive photographed near Moran, Ohio. Passenger service, however, was abandoned in 1938.

ALONG THE WABASH

The two action shots on the right illustrate the versatility of modern steam motive power. Both locomotives are giant Mountain-types from the Wabash's 2800 series, one hauling a heavy drag freight and the other wheeling a crack passenger limited. No. 2820 in the upper photograph is rolling along at 75 with the Banner Blue Limited, the blue-painted, fast schedule varnish on the day run between Chicago and St. Louis, a coach and Pullman luxury train that is the pride of the road. In the lower photograph No. 2822 powers a heavy drag freight and was caught with white flags flying eastbound out of Springfield, Illinois. These handsome and utilitarian engines are at home at any speed up to 85 miles an hour and with any load up to 150 reefers.

Lucius Bee

THE CHEYENNE MAIL

Hustling into Denver with a cloud of road-bed dust and cinders in its wake, the Union Pacific's Cheyenne Mail is powered by an old-type, high boiler Pacific, No. 2897, with an extra length of sleeve on her smoke-stack. Below is an aged American-type 4-4-0 in service on the Boston and Maine between Boston and Reading Highlands with a train of old-time open platform coaches.

Lucius Bee

Lucius Beebe

STORMING DOWN THE PANHANDLE

A few miles north of Amarillo, Texas, the crack varnish, No. 1, of the Fort Worth and Denver City (Burlington) heads toward Fort Worth and Dallas behind heavy Pacific No. 2971. The Burlington's access to Texas is over the iron of the Colorado and Southern out of Denver and continues into the Lone Star State over the Fort Worth and Denver City.

much difficulty, but they run most efficiently at about 55. To hit 90 or more, their load has to be reduced substantially.

In the case of the Mountain or 4-8-2 types, which in a sense are enlarged Pacific-types, the ratio of tractive force to weight is about six to one, or about 14 per cent lower than for the Pacific-type. This indicates the 4-8-2s cannot pull their heaviest loads nearly so swiftly as the 4-6-2s. Which is precisely the case; the power inherent in the former is aimed at hauling even heavier trains less swiftly. Working with a heavy passenger train, they are doing well to attain 70, and are operated most efficiently at speeds of 45 to 55. With a smaller train they can easily surpass 70.

As for the freight engines, the heavy 2-10-2 is simply a bigger version of the light 2-10-2, which in turn is a larger edition of the heavy 2-8-2, which is the same thing, only bigger, as the light 2-8-2. The ratios in each are practically the same; and each could perform, with its rated trains, about the same under the same conditions. Considering their weight, they can start tremendous loads, but have reached their efficient speed with those loads at about 40 miles an hour, and have to strain themselves to achieve 60. Again, a lighter train will allow each of them to go faster.

At this point it may be wise to define what is meant by rated load or heaviest load, which have been used interchangeably. It does not designate the heaviest train an engine can start on level, straight track; no engine could run very far with such a burden. Rather, it represents the heaviest load the locomotive can start and handle easily over the grades and curves of the average division over which it is expected to run. The speed of an unburdened steam locomotive is practically unlimited; on good track it theoretically can go on accelerating until its cylinders are using all the steam its boiler can make. Actually, it would have disintegrated before it ever got to that point. And the smaller its driving-wheels, the more quickly it would have pounded itself to pieces. There is nothing inherent in the steam-engine to limit its speed; the problem is just how much to compromise speed with pulling power.

In addition to those mentioned, there were U.S.R.A. designs for switchers and Mallets. Since the principles of the former have not changed in years, and since the latter are no more than giant editions of the former, they can be dismissed. The types under consideration represent effectively the locomotives which hauled America's trains in their best development up till 1925, and a generality can be established with the observation that passenger engines were designed to operate at scheduled speeds of little more than 70 miles an hour, and freight engines at 45 or 50. In terms of loads, a 150-ton passenger locomotive (say 250 tons with tender loaded) was expected to handle a thousand tons or more of coaches and Pullmans; and a 175-ton freight locomotive (perhaps 275 tons with tender loaded) was expected to roll down the line with five or six thousand tons of box-cars. They still are, too.

Standard U.S.R.A. light Pacific-types are pulling main line passenger expresses on the Atlantic Coast Line, Louisville and Nashville, Baltimore and Ohio, and others; and the U.S.R.A. heavy Pacifics or their equivalent are assigned to such as the Erie Limited, the Pennsy's whole fleet of limiteds, the Chicago and North Western's 400, the Lehigh Valley's Black Diamond, the Katy's Bluebonnet. The Southern Pacific's Sunbeam's brand-new streamlined trains on a non-stop schedule between Dallas and Houston, Texas, are handled by rebuilt Pacifics which are a sort of sublimation of the U.S.R.A. 4-6-2s.

The dominant characteristic of new locomotive design is more speed, both in passenger and freight service. Engines must be able to cruise with a regular passenger train at 90 miles an hour, and to surpass 100 with comparative ease. Freight locomotives must be able to ramble along at 65 or 70 with substantial pay-loads. Thanks again to its simplicity, the steam locomotive could easily be adjusted for such service: the boiler and fire-box simply had to be built proportionately larger than they had been. Not merely larger, it will be noted, but proportionately larger; the size and capacity of the boiler had to be increased in greater measure than the starting tractive force.

The first outstanding evidence of the new order in passenger engines appeared in the shape of the New York Central's Hudson or 4-6-4 type, back in 1926. The design itself was probably some years older, and was not entirely a New York Central development, either, since the motive power designers of other roads and locomotive companies had the same sort of thing in mind or on paper. In 1925, the Chesapeake and Ohio purchased five Pacific-type engines from the American Locomotive Company, whose dimensions, which included 80 square feet of grate and an unprecedented amount of heating surface, are in line with the best modern practice. These engines, Nos. 490-494, are used to haul the George Washington and the Sportsman.

The New York Central was the logical place for the development of an engine distinguished for steaming capacity at high speed. Because of its water-level route, its passenger locomotives always have been planned for comparatively low tractive force rating, with the emphasis on speed. Its last Pacific-type, the K-5, turned out in 1925, is a very modern engine; and, in fact, is used to haul the streamlined Mercury between Cleveland and Detroit. And one of the main reasons for the evolution of the Hudson-type was to haul heavier trains rather than to wheel them more swiftly. When the new locomotives went into operation, however, the New York Central found itself with a machine capable not only of handling heavier trains, but of achieving considerably higher speeds with them.

The best chart of the improvement in engine design is afforded by comparing the main dimensions of the Hudson with those of the U.S.R.A. heavy Pacific:

	HUDSON, FIRST SERIES	PACIFIC
Cylinders	25 x 28 in.	27 x 28 in.
Drivers	79 in.	79 in.
Pressure	225 lbs.	200 lbs.
Weight on drivers	182,000 lbs.	197,000 lbs.
Total weight	350,000 lbs.	306,000 lbs.
Combined heating surface . .	6,425 sq. ft.	4,711 sq. ft.
Grate	82 sq. ft.	71 sq. ft.
Tractive force	42,300 lbs.	43,900 lbs.

Here, in a few figures, is the specific evidence of ten years' progress in locomotives. Though the Hudson is heavier and more powerful by far, as a comparison of the boiler dimensions instantly makes clear, its tractive force rating is actually less. Its ratio of total weight to tractive force is about eight to one, compared to seven to one for the U.S.R.A. machine, and it carries much less of its weight on its drivers. The Hudson uses its increased steaming capacity not to start more cars, but to move them more swiftly—to roll its heaviest load 75 miles an hour easily and efficiently, and to push above 90 without trouble. Tests have shown that it develops its maximum horse-power at close to 80 miles an hour, with a huge train of cars, whereas the U.S.R.A. 4-6-2 does so between 50 and 55 miles an hour. In regular service, between New York and Chicago, it pulls 18 Pullmans on practically mile-a-minute running time, and has been timed wheeling 21 cars over the Michigan Central at more than 80 miles an hour.

Naturally, it was evident that starting tractive force no longer was a dominant indication of a locomotive's ability. What really counted was tractive force at speed. To give a clearer idea of that, locomotive men began to talk in terms of horse-power again. For a long time they had shied clear of assigning a horse-power rating to a steam locomotive, not only because tractive force presented a more optimistic account of its power, but, since speed is an element in horse-power, it was hard to compute accurately. With the new design, though, they had to refrain from exploiting tractive force figures. And figuring horse-power wasn't easy. There was a cylinder horse-power formula which didn't concern itself with boiler size, and invariably underestimated the capacity of a modern engine; and there was a boiler horse-power formula which was of practically prohibitive complexity. About the most trustworthy way of estimating horse-power, it was finally decided, was to test the engine in actual service. Many of these tests established the circumstance that the horse-power of a modern engine, that is, one with an ample fire-box and boiler, may be determined roughly by multiplying the grate area by 500. In the case of the N.Y.C. Hudson-types it works out exactly; road tests at 66 miles an hour showed something like 4100 horse-power, and the engines have 81 square feet of grate.

Even so, horse-power estimates incline to be very conservative. The Lackawanna's new 4-6-4s, which at least are equal to the N.Y.C. engines, are rated at around 3600 horse-power; and other railroads are just as modest about their arbitrary ratings.

What the 4-6-4 did for New York Central passenger service was done

Lucius Beeb

almost immediately, on an even more intense scale, for freight and passenger service all over the country. To-day the Hudson-type has been improved (but made no bigger) on the N.Y.C. with a fleet of 50 new engines (ten of which are streamlined and are hauling the Twentieth Century and other mile-a-minute trains), and larger versions of the same idea are to be found elsewhere. The most striking are those of the Santa Fe, Chicago and North Western, and Milwaukee, the last of which use 300 pounds of boiler pressure, develop 4500 or more horse-power, have 84-inch driving-wheels, and weigh more than 200 tons without tenders. These great machines, which carry only about half their weight on their drivers, are proportioned so that they develop their maximum horse-power at better than 80 miles an hour, and are cruising along nicely, as engine builders now say, at 80 or 90. The Santa Fe uses its five new 4-6-4s to pull The Chief on a 49-hour schedule between Chicago and Los Angeles (the 4-6-4s work only between Chicago and La Junta), and occasionally to pinch-hit for the Diesel-electric on the Super Chief, which is about nine hours swifter. The Chicago and North Western employs its nine new Hudsons to handle its swiftest expresses between Chicago and Omaha, and on the 400, between Chicago and Minneapolis. Though the Milwaukee's four were not completed when this was written, they will turn out to be of the same general dimensions as the Santa Fe and North Western designs, and will be assigned to the road's crack trains.

Speaking of the Milwaukee Road brings to mind the original Hiawatha locomotives, which perhaps have more in common with the largest Hudsons than with those of the N.Y.C. and others of their general capacity. The first two were completed in the spring of 1935 and immediately installed on the Hiawatha, in competition with the Burlington's two Diesel-electric streamliners and the Chicago and North Western's steam-powered 400, all on the same schedule. As modern engine design goes, the Hiawatha locomotives represent nearly as distinct an advance over the N.Y.C. Hudsons as the Hudsons were over the older Pacifics. Designed for even greater cruising speeds than the 4-6-4s, they actually develop their maximum horse-power, which is about 3000, between 90 and 100 miles an hour. They were the first serious attempts to meet the competition of the Diesel-electrics, and thus were intended to haul no heavier train than a 3000-horse-power Diesel-electric. This was an important item; there are plenty of 3000-horse-power passenger engines running to-day which pull three times the load normally assigned to a Diesel-electric of the same rating. So these Hiawatha engines were rather small, weighing 290,000 pounds and exerting only 30,700 pounds of starting tractive force. Since they run over heavy rails and a first-class road-bed, the Milwaukee managed to keep the number of axles down to five, and made a 4-4-2 or Atlantic-type out of them—the first Atlantic-types in years, at just about the time when the 4-4-2 wheel arrangement was considered definitely obsolete.

These machines have 84-inch driving-wheels, 300 pounds of pressure, and enough grate and heating surface to generate steam for continued acceleration at 100 miles an hour. In many ways, their design was more daring than that of the Hudsons, which stemmed from the amply-proportioned 4-6-2s before them. The Milwaukee Road and American Locomotive Company had nothing much to go by except a concept, and plenty of experience. But railroad men often have seen theoretically marvelous engines turn out to be unqualified failures, and, while the dimensions of these 4-4-2s were worked out carefully and the engines kept as simple as possible, nobody could predict what might happen. Too, nearly every new type usually has been given the benefit of extended trials before being proclaimed to the world, whereas these had to be placed in regular service almost immediately.

But they rolled out of the Schenectady shops nearly perfect in every detail. Nothing had to be changed, no proportion had to be altered. As a cautious gesture, the American Locomotive Company had not guaranteed them to maintain their fast schedule with six cars—about the same load (a little less than 400 tons) as the one for which the Diesel-electric people were designing their 3000-horse-power machines. Once on the run, though, the Hiawathas performed so satisfactorily that another car or two was added. A little more than a year later, each was regularly pulling nine cars averaging about 50 tons apiece.

With several unevenly-spaced stops, the schedule of the Hiawatha is one of the most exacting in all railroading. During the summer of 1936 it was carded to cover the 85 miles between Milwaukee and Chicago in 70 minutes (a 73-mile average), during which it was actually scheduled to run at 102 miles an hour. (Now on 75-minute running time, it generally does the 85 miles in 70 minutes and sometimes in less. Once it did so in 63 minutes.) It was also expected to cover the 43.1 miles between New Lisbon and Portage, Wisconsin, from a dead start at New Lisbon, in 34 minutes, including time out for the stop at Portage. This called for an average of 76 or 77 miles an hour. The train is placed under no speed restriction; its engineers are cautioned, in the official time-card, not to surpass certain speeds at certain places, such as slowing down to 90 on some curves. Not long ago on an exactingly clocked Chicago to

St. Paul run, the Hiawatha exceeded 100 miles an hour at six different points; and, delayed several times, covered the 410 miles of its haul in less than 350 minutes of running time. Taking everything together, these 4-4-2 engines are probably the world's swiftest locomotives of any kind. What is most important, they are earning money to the reputed extent of a million net dollars a year for the Milwaukee Road.

As for other roads, they have gone in for Hudson-types of the same general proportions as the N.Y.C. engines. Standard 4-6-4s are running on the Canadian National, Canadian Pacific, Milwaukee, Burlington, and Santa Fe. The Baltimore and Ohio has constructed a smaller 4-6-4 which it has named the Lord Baltimore (the first with 84-inch drivers), and which was used on the first Royal Blue; and the Maine Central and Nickel Plate also have installed a few of considerably smaller size. In addition, the Frisco and Illinois Central have gone in for some home-made models, using the boilers of older engines. The Frisco's ten 4-6-4s furnish a nice lesson in the development of the modern steam locomotive. They were built a score of years ago as 4-6-2s with 63 square feet of grate. Unwilling to admit they were completely worn out, but willing enough to agree they weren't proportioned in the best modern fashion, the Frisco simply tore off their fire-boxes and reconstructed the back end of the boiler, installing a vast fire-box with $82\frac{1}{2}$ square feet of grate. As rebuilt, the engines boasted very little increase in starting tractive force, but considerably more steaming capacity, and hence the ability to travel more swiftly, easily and economically with the same train. The change nearly doubled the weight on the trailing truck, which had to be replaced with a four-wheel arrangement. And there is illustrated the essential difference between the 4-6-2 and the 4-6-4 type.

With the exception of two somewhat experimental engines, the Pennsylvania Railroad, as we've already noted, has developed no new steam locomotive exclusively for passenger trains in more than 20 years. Its famous and handsome K-4s, which have very little, if any, more power than the U.S.R.A. 4-6-2, are not capable of hauling anywhere near as much as the N.Y.C. Hudsons at high speed, though they do have a greater tractive force rating. Between Harrisburg and Pittsburgh, around the curves and up the hills of the Alleghenies, where almost any engine would have to be double-headed with a heavy train, this discrepancy is not so important; engines need more pulling power under 50 miles an hour than they do with plenty of steam at 75. But farther westward, where schedules demand averages of nearly 75 miles an hour, for hundreds of miles on end, the K-4 cannot handle nearly so many cars as it used to at 55- and 60-mile averages. And though it was never intended to run 90 miles an hour in ordinary service, it does so every day, which is a prodigious tribute to the steam locomotive. Probably no other locomotive has so great a capacity for surpassing its own requirements.

Meantime, the Baltimore and Ohio, which, over a period of 20 years, has experimented with more different types and kinds of motive power than any other road in the country, has a 200-ton 4-4-4-4 type on the rails, hauling both freight and passenger trains. The reason for this rather drastic wheel arrangement in these days of strong track is easy to arrive at. When the enormous main and side-rods of a heavy engine are traveling up and down (often more than 300 times a minute), what is known as dynamic augment is set up. Since the rods on one side necessarily follow those on the other by only a quarter of a turn, and since the counterweights (the crescent-shaped pieces opposite the pins of the drivers) more than compensate for the weight of the pins and rods, the wheels tend to lift up and come down on the rails once every revolution.

But this dynamic augment is not the important consideration it used to be. Improvement in the running-gear of newer engines, steam men assert, has reduced dynamic augment to the point where the steam locomotive need be no harder on the tracks than a Diesel-electric of the same capacity. Lighter rods and roller-bearing assemblies, and especially disk-type driving-wheels, are responsible. Perhaps a tear ought to be shed for the passing of the old spoked driving-wheels, which usually seemed higher than they were, and certainly gave locomotives a light-footed air the solid driving-wheels do not. William Mason, who once called disk-type leading truck-wheels cheesy because they looked like cheeses, would no doubt be grieved by the new drivers if he were living to-day.

In the case of the B.&O. and Pennsy, the latter of which has the heavier track and can stand more dynamic augment than almost any other railroad, still another thing was responsible for the 4-4-4-4 wheel arrangement: the necessity for getting around sharp curves. Four connected driving-wheels, the Pennsy found, couldn't be over 72 inches in diameter if they were to run satisfactorily around the sharp Allegheny curves. A really high-capacity, high-speed machine would need four of about 80-inch diameter.

Though this brief consideration is categorically unconcerned with eccentric designs, it can spare a few words for the Baltimore and Ohio's projected constant torque steam-engine, and the steam-electric machine of the Union Pacific. The former is the equivalent of a 5000-horse-power 4-8-4 except that the driving-wheels are not connected. Each driving axle is powered by a separate four-cylinder steam motor, making 16 cylinders in all; and the possibilities for trouble are compensated for by the fact that each pair of drivers and its motor can be removed on a drop pit in a few minutes. While it is more complicated and expensive to build than a regular steam locomotive of its power, it does away with dynamic augment, uneven starting, and slow acceleration at very low speeds; and it is vastly lighter and simpler than a Diesel-electric of the same capacity. The Union Pacific engine is of about the same rating. It is similar to a Diesel except that a steam turbine, powered by an extremely efficient flash boiler which can raise a full head of steam in a phenomenally short time, runs the dynamos generating the electricity for the power trucks. It is equipped with condensers which change the exhaust-steam back into water, and thus can run hundreds of miles without taking water. But it is staggeringly expensive—fully as expensive, in fact, as a Diesel-electric. It costs to build around $650,000, or more than four times the price of a heavy 4-8-4 type steam engine.

First turned out in 1911, the 4-8-2 or Mountain-type found wide favor for 20 years. Though the U.S.R.A. model was better fitted for hauling fairly heavy trains at medium speed, the 4-8-2 made a satisfactory passenger engine, and was often developed more in that direction by being fitted with larger drivers than the 69-inch wheels of the U.S.R.A. engines, and by having its ratios altered somewhat. In the West, where none of the passenger trains ran as swiftly as the New York–Chicago flyers, it was the most popular engine for heavy passenger service. The Rock Island, Great Northern, Union Pacific, Santa Fe, Southern Pacific,

Missouri Pacific, and several of the Southern roads also adopted it. Most of them still use it. Even the Forty-niner, the only all-Pullman stream-liner to San Francisco, is hauled on the Union Pacific by a shrouded (i.e., streamlined) Mountain-type, and on the Southern Pacific by one of its 4300 series of 4-8-2s. The same goes for the Overland. In addition, 4-8-2s are handling the Missouri Pacific's Sunshine Special and City of Mexico, some of the Pennsy's crack main-line trains, the Illinois Central's Panama Limited, and the Chicago-to-Florida expresses operating over the Louisville and Nashville, to say nothing of practically all of the Southern Pacific main-line passenger trains.

The 4-8-2 also proved to be a life-saver in fast freight service. With a starting tractive force rating the same as that of the light Mikado, the standard U.S.R.A. Mountain-type obviously can handle a very heavy freight train. Once having started it, it can achieve a pace quite impossible for the Mikado, since its boiler and fire-box and drivers are all larger than those of the Mikado.

About the time the 4-6-2 was being enlarged into the 4-6-4, plans were made to do the same thing to the 4-8-2, and in 1927 the 4-8-4 wheel arrangement appeared on the Santa Fe, Canadian National, Northern Pacific, and Lackawanna. In most cases, these engines developed very little more tractive force, but showed a vast increase in boiler and fire-box dimensions. They carried less of their total weight on their drivers, and generally used higher boiler pressure and smaller cylinders. Compared to the heavy U.S.R.A. 4-8-2, the average 4-8-4 being constructed to-day has about 25 per cent more grate area, heating surface, and total weight, but only 12 per cent increase in rated tractive force. Here again is concise evidence of the new design, with its emphasis on steaming power at speed.

And so, while the U.S.R.A. machines were fitted only for rather slow passenger service—say a night train between two cities 400 miles apart, or a long, unhurried haul over hills and around curves—the new 4-8-4s can be used either in fast freight or the swiftest passenger service. A 4-8-4 like the ones on the Union Pacific, Northern Pacific, or Richmond, Fredericksburg and Potomac can roll along at 75 or 80 miles with 20 standard Pullmans and not be harassed in the slightest; it can pick up

a hundred loaded box-cars and wheel them at a pace which would have been thought daring for a passenger train only as long ago as 1921. Indeed, some freight trains these days are being operated more swiftly than many passenger trains on the same line. The railroads competing for the overnight New York and Jersey to Buffalo business high-ball merchandise trains from terminus to terminus at an average of more than 40 miles an hour, including all stops; the Cotton Belt's Blue Streak rattles down through Arkansas to reach Pine Bluff only 10 hours after leaving St. Louis, 400 miles to the north. And the Illinois Central's MS-1 (pulled by a home-made 4-8-2) requires less than 13 hours to cover the 528 miles between Chicago and Memphis, outrunning the Floridian and overtaking the Louisiane, the night express to Memphis and New Orleans, both first-class passenger trains.

The bewildering thing about the 4-8-4 type is that its type alone tells nothing of what it is going to be used for. Judging it by the size of the driver diameter, an old and fairly trustworthy if not very scientific rule-of-thumb, indicates nothing at all, because one railroad may use an engine with large drivers in freight service, while its neighbor will assign a 4-8-4 with smaller wheels to a passenger train. The Soo Line uses some 4-8-4's with 75-inch driving-wheels for its freights between Chicago and the Twin Cities; but the Southern Pacific employs streamlined 4-8-4s of about the same dimensions but with only 73-inch drivers to wheel its fast and flashy Daylight, between San Francisco and Los Angeles. Again, the Milwaukee Road recently bought a fleet of 30 giant 4-8-4s to displace 55 Mikados in freight service. Though they are considered to be freight locomotives, they are also intended for the transcontinental Olympian, on the 914-mile run between Minneapolis and Harlowton, Montana, when the train operates with 18 or 20 cars. Compared to their predecessors, the U.S.R.A. heavy Mikados, they show a 48 per cent increase in weight, 51 per cent increase in grate area, and only 12 per cent increase in starting tractive force. Here is an even more compelling example of what is happening to railroad engines than that afforded by comparing the 4-8-4 with the U.S.R.A. 4-8-2.

Mr. Samuel Vauclain, of the Baldwin Works, is convinced that the day will come when engines with 80-inch drivers, employed only for the swiftest passenger engines of the middle twenties, will be hauling freight trains. The Great Northern, Southern Pacific, and Santa Fe already have managed to put 80-inch drivers under a 4-8-4 type, but have assigned them exclusively to passenger service. There is no urgent reason why they couldn't be used for freight trains; and of course driving-wheels only a couple of inches smaller are rolling freight every day. Mr. Vauclain may live to see his prediction come true. By then it will be a relatively unimportant circumstance; modern 4-8-4s have already reached the point where they are dual-service machines in every respect.

But only 12 or 14 per cent of the railroads' revenues come from passenger trains, and only a fraction of the freight really must be dispatched at a mile a minute. About half the national freight tonnage is mine products, most of which can be hauled at whatever speed is cheapest and most convenient. One might be justified in inferring, then, that the new design has not been applied to heavy freight engines. Nevertheless, it has. The old-time hog, the crawling, heaving, smoke-belching drag freight engine of 20 years ago, is being replaced by engines which also have proportionately more steaming ability at speed. Improving the freight engine, too, was not merely a matter of enlarging it; the Santa Fe or 2-10-2 type was in effect a swollen 2-8-2, and the only respect in which it surpassed the 2-8-2 was its ability to haul greater pay-loads. What happened was that both the 2-8-2 and the 2-10-2 were converted into different types by application of the new principles in the form of a larger fire-box and hence a four-wheel trailing truck under it: the 2-8-2 became the 2-8-4, and the 2-10-2 became the 2-10-4.

Surprisingly, this occurred before the 4-6-2 was changed to the 4-6-4. The Lima Works, which led in developing the so-called super-power locomotives, completed the first 2-8-4 in 1925. Tried out on the Boston and Albany, it became known as the Berkshire-type, after the Berkshire Hills of Massachusetts, on whose grades it achieved its initial success. That year Lima also completed the first real 2-10-4 or Texas-type for the Texas and Pacific, which donated part of its name to the wheel arrangement. Technically, the first 2-10-4 appeared on the Santa Fe in 1919, when a four-wheel truck was installed under the fire-box of a standard 2-10-2 engine. Actually, it was not a true 2-10-4 type at all, having little in common with the better-designed engine of 1925.

Since 1925, locomotives of both types not only have become popular, but have been improved considerably. The Erie bought some enormous 2-8-4s with 70-inch driving-wheels in 1927 which turned out to be superb machines, and within a very few years 105 of them were on the Erie's tracks. About that time the Chesapeake and Ohio, watching their success, started to consider the same principle in a larger engine—that is, a 2-10-4 with large driving-wheels. Now, the C. & O. is a coal road; it hauls huge trains of coal at low cost per ton-mile. For such trains it owned hundreds of low-speed, high-powered, articulated engines, among which were 35 less than six years old.

But by 1928 it was convinced that even the coal-hauling engine of the future needed to be redesigned, and after experimenting with one of the Erie 2-8-4s, ordered 40 of the 2-10-4 type. They had 69-inch driving-wheels and weighed 566,000 pounds, and still are the world's largest and most powerful two-cylinder steam locomotives. Again, they have no more starting tractive force than the older 2-8-8-2 articulated engines; what they can do is wheel the same load (10,000 tons or better) more swiftly and economically. Lately there has been a small boom in this style: the Kansas City Southern and the Santa Fe have bought ten apiece, while the Bessemer and Lake Erie, whose motive power always has been designed for great pulling power at low speed, has increased its roster of 2-10-4s to 30 engines.

Obviously the small-wheeled 2-10-2 type has been dated, though some roads cannot, however, subscribe to the fact while they still have them on hand. One or two lines have sold theirs, while at least two others, the Frisco and the Illinois Central, have been rebuilding theirs into 4-8-2 type machines, for fast freight trains.

Even the articulated locomotive has been redesigned. This type, which flourished as a Mallet compound during the U.S.R.A. period, was intended for heavy, slow trains—for pushing other trains up the mountains or for hauling enormous drags of iron or coal at a steady crawl. The Virginian "Triplex" Mallet (which had three sets of drivers and six cylinders) was built with a theoretical tractive force rating of nearly 200,000 pounds, and could therefore start more than any steam locomotive before or since; but its boiler capacity was exhausted before it was doing 15 miles an hour with its heaviest practicable train.

The trend away from such lumbering, phlegmatic monsters seems also to have started in 1925, with the construction of some 2-8-8-2 type articulated engines for the Great Northern. They were not merely pusher engines, but main line freight locomotives—not intended to run at 70 miles an hour, to be sure, but at least capable of maintaining a reasonable average with a big train over heavy grades. So the articulated engine was revived; and by 1929 the Northern Pacific was operating its gigantic 2-8-8-4 locomotive, the heaviest, largest and (on a horse-power basis) probably the most powerful steam locomotive ever built, to pull 4000-ton

SMOKE, STEAM AND GLORY AT SUMMIT

Caught by the cameraman behind Atchison, Topeka and Santa Fe locomotives 3531 and 3724, the Grand Canyon Limited mounts to the highest point in the Cajon Pass in the San Bernardino Mountains of California, presenting a railroad picture only infrequently recorded.

INTO DENVER YARDS

Union Pacific Train 38, the Pony Express, eastbound, with 15 mail-cars, coaches and Pullmans, pulls into Denver with cars from San Francisco, Los Angeles, Seattle and Portland to be set out at Denver, Kansas City and St. Louis. The heavy Mountain locomotive with simplified lines, disk drivers and pumps shielded in behind the pilot beam is typical of U.P. passenger motive power on its long western hauls.

INTO THE MAIN

Upper left:
Lucius Beebe
With his Johnson bar notched well forward, the driver of the Baltimore and Ohio's Wayne Junction–Chicago Mail, No. 13, wheels his heavy Pacific, No. 5303, over the switch points just south of the Chestnut Street Station, Philadelphia.

HOT SHOT NORTH

Lower left:
Lucius Beebe
April sees the heaviest freight movements of the year over the rails of the Texas and Pacific, for at this season in addition to the regular petroleum and agricultural products of Texas and the bananas and Caribbean importations from Gulf ports, the movement of cattle from South Texas to the northern ranges reaches its peak. Sometimes a thousand cars roll into Fort Worth and are sent north and west in five hours. Here is a fast extra bound for Kansas City rolling along the outside track past the T.&P. terminal at Fort Worth in the tow of a powerful 2-10-2 or Santa Fe–type engine.

Railroad Photograph

SEABOARD FREIGHT

A Canadian Pacific heavy freight Mikado, No. 5386, battling the grade at Field
Hill near Yoho, British Columbia, with the brakeman riding the pilot to throw a
loop switch higher up the line.

UP SHERMAN HILL

Two Union Pacific monsters, a 2-8-8-0 and a 2-10-2, slamming their exhausts
skyward as they tackle the Sherman Hill grade with a hundred-odd carloads of
mixed freight strung out behind them.

Railroad Photograph

POWER ON THE DENVER AND RIO GRANDE WESTERN

From Denver to Salt Lake City by way of the fabled Moffat Tunnel and some of the most spectacular railroading in the world and the Dotsero Cut-off, the Denver and Rio Grande Western saves 140 miles by going over and through the Colorado Rockies instead of around them. The road's other route by way of the Royal Gorge, Colorado Springs and Pueblo is almost as magnificent and the photograph shows train No. 1, the Scenic Limited, pulling out of Denver Union Station early in the morning on the south and westbound run. The 1800 series of Denver and Rio Grande Western locomotives includes five Baldwin-built dual-service type 4-8-4s. They have 26 by 30-inch cylinders, 72-inch drivers, 285 pounds pressure, weigh 476,360 pounds, exert 67,000 pounds tractive force and develop 5000 horse-power. They cost $140,000 apiece and are used to haul the road's crack freight and passenger trains on both Moffat Tunnel and Royal Gorge runs.

THE GULF COAST LIMITED

Hauled by a Richmond, Fredericksburg and Potomac Super-Pacific with its pumps and exhaust-heater jacket mounted on the smoke box, the Atlantic Coast Line's No. 74, the Gulf Coast Limited, rolls over the R.F.&P.'s iron on the Richmond-Washington run. Operating during the winter months in conjunction with the Florida East Coast, the R.F.&P., the Pennsylvania and the New Haven, the Gulf Coast Limited sets out and picks up Pullmans over the greater part of the Atlantic seaboard and is one of the crack trains serving the luxury resorts of Florida during the season. H. W. Pontin snapped No. 308 with a leash of fifteen Pullmans doing better than a mile a minute headed north between Milford and Fredericksburg.

DOUBLE-SHOTTED FREIGHT

With 180 carloads of coal in tow, these two Chesapeake and Ohio hogs, super 2-8-2 and 2-10-4 types coupled, are dragging out of Columbus, Ohio, on an eastern run.

THUNDER AT TWILIGHT

A Colorado and Southern fast freight at Walsenburg, Colorado, as night is falling. The locomotive is a Santa Fe–type, No. 908, hauling a hot consist with stock-cars on the head of the train.

THE ARCHETYPAL AMERICAN 4-4-0

The most successful and longest lived of any type of steam locomotive ever used on American railroads is the classic eight-wheeler with two pairs of coupled driving-wheels and a four-wheeled leading truck. From 1836, when it was patented by Henry R. Campbell, chief engineer of the Philadelphia, Germantown and Norristown Railroad, down to the present, when many eight-wheelers are still in service on short hauls and branch roads, the American-type engine has been the standard motive power from which all other types have derived. The first of its breed had 54-inch drivers, weighed about 12 tons and had a tractive power of 4480 pounds. It had inside cylinders whose pistons were connected to a crank axle on the lead pair of drivers and carried a deep fire-box slung between the driving axles. Through innumerable mutations and improvements of design the eight-wheeler retained its essential characteristics and for many decades was the standard product of such noted works as Baldwin, Breese and Kneeland, William Mason, Rogers, Ketchem and Grosvenor, Taunton, Richard Norris and McKay and Aldus. Until the development of the Atlantic-type loco-motive with its higher horse-power and economy of fuel consumption sealed the doom of the eight-wheeler it was king of the American iron. The photograph shows a Baldwin 4-4-0, No. 296, of the Virginian, leaving Victoria, Virginia, on the Roanoke-Norfolk run.

Lucius Beebe

ON THE OUTSIDE IRON

THE VAUDREUIL MAIL

On the Montreal-Ottawa run, the Canadian Pacific's light Pacific, No. 2217, leaves Windsor Station with two cars of His Majesty's mails and a brace of passenger-coaches. Vaudreuil is west of Montreal on the Point Fortune–Ottawa line.

"IN YELLOW FIELDS OF ASPHODEL"

In deepest New England the St. Johnsbury and Lake Champlain's No. 38, a 2-8-0 type, rolls across the meadows near Wolcott, Vermont. In the background is one of the few remaining covered bridges for which the Yankee country-side is celebrated in rural legend. Fifty years ago wooden covered bridges were common in the east but fire and steel construction rendered their picturesqueness obsolete.

CORN KING, FOURTH SECTION

The first western railroad to direct its operations by telegraph and the first road to build a railway postal-car, the Chicago and North Western was largely built by English capital and is to-day the only railroad in the United States whose trains drive on the left side of the road instead of the right. A six-hundred-million-dollar system with more than 10,000 miles of main line trackage, the North Western has other pioneering firsts to its credit: it ran the first Pullman sleeping-cars west of Chicago, it instituted the first through dining-car service to San Francisco and, in conjunction with the Union Pacific and Southern Pacific, it runs an almost continuous line of double rails two-thirds of the distance across the North American continent. The above photograph shows Train 22, the Corn King, drawn by No. 3016, a 4-8-4 type, pulling into Lake Street, Chicago, on the run east from Omaha.

WESTBOUND OUT OF OMAHA

The first section of the Challenger, one of the Union Pacific's fleet which heads out of the Nebraska terminal for the open prairie with the rising sun every morning. Inaugurated in 1935 as a medium-priced means of rail transport between Chicago and Los Angeles, the Challenger at once became so popular as to require the conversion of a vast quantity of equipment to supply extra sections and established itself as the best money-maker of the U.P.'s passenger trains. Over its 2,298-mile route it averages better than 40 miles an hour, comparing favorably with all but such extra-fare limiteds as the City of Los Angeles and the Santa Fe's Super Chief. Harmoniously decorated, and scientifically lighted and ventilated, the Challenger is made up of the most modern coaches with tourist sleepers which only a few years since were standard equipment. Like the U.P. streamliners, the Challenger was the suggestion of the U.P.'s chairman, W. Averell Harriman.

SUPERPOWER ON THE PENNSY

This Pennsylvania way-freight heading east out of Canton, Ohio, is double-shotted with a Super 2-10-0 capable of a tractive effort of 90,000 pounds leading a 2-10-2 over the switch points with a mixed consist. A remarkably suggestive photograph of steam-power rolling down the illimitable iron.

TEST RUN

This Chesapeake and Ohio Super 2-10-4, No. 3003, the world's most powerful two-cylinder simple-type locomotive, is shown about to cross the Erie diamond at Marion, Ohio, bound for Russell, Kentucky, hauling a test-train of 210 cars.

THE GREEN AND GOLD OF THE SOUTHERN

With a spread eagle mounted above the green lacquer of its boiler shell, light Pacific No. 1363 of the Southern Railway heads the Birmingham Special into Alexandria, Virginia, on the southbound run.

INTO THE ALEXANDRIA YARDS

The Southern Railway's Mikado, No. 4817, running ahead of a mile of hotshot freight from the Florida citrus groves, heads into the yards at Alexandria, Virginia, just over the line from Washington, whence, after classification, the greater part of its cars will continue north behind the power of the Pennsylvania.

FAST MAIL ALONG THE ESPEE

Compensating in power and adaptability for what they lack in sightliness, the Southern Pacific's cab-first Super-Mallets were designed by Baldwin to give the engine driver clear vision and protection when operating around sharp curves and through tunnels and snow-sheds on mountain divisions. The Southern Pacific has more than seventy of these monsters in operation and they are familiar sights above Sacramento into the Sierras. They are 125 feet in length, weigh, with tender loaded, 1,028,700 pounds and have a tractive force of 124,300 pounds with a horse-power of 6,000 at 40 miles an hour. The action photograph shows the first section of the West Coast Mail, Train No. 60 (carrying green), heading into Los Angeles ahead of fourteen cars of freight and passengers.

ROLLING DOWN THE CALIFORNIA MILES

This Santa Fe 4-6-0 muzzle-loader used to haul the Los Angeles–San Bernardino local through the orange groves and vineyards of lower California, a route laid through the back yards of innumerable suburban villas and a hundred grade crossings. To-day the run is handled with a motor train and No. 493 is in service somewhere along the desert stretches of Arizona and New Mexico.

Railroad Photographs

POWER ON THE NORFOLK AND WESTERN

On its maiden haul, the Norfolk and Western's latest 1937 model 2-6-6-4 with 120 cars of mixed freight behind her is shown southbound out of Columbus, Ohio. Note the light-weight rods and motion, the stay bolts on the piston-heads and the size of the fire-box with its consequent sustained steaming capacity.

G. M. Best

DOUBLE-HEADED FOR LEADVILLE

Behind two of the Colorado and Southern's narrow-gage engines equipped with smoke-deflectors which pipe part of the exhaust down to the tracks, this seven-car mail and passenger train is heading out of Denver for Leadville, high in the Colorado Rockies. The Colorado and Southern's narrow gage shares in the fragrant tradition of the Denver and Rio Grande, the Virginia and Truckee and the other small span lines of the old West so precious to the frontier legend.

ROLLING NORTH TO FRISCO

This Southern Pacific 2-8-2, No. 3305, formerly an E.P.&S.W. locomotive, is heading north out of Los Angeles with 90 cars of mixed freight.

Railroad Photographs

THE NICKEL PLATE LIMITED

The New York, Chicago and St. Louis Railroad, known as the Nickel Plate
Road, schedules few passenger hauls, the bulk of its traffic being the freight of
industrial Michigan and Ohio and the produce of Indiana and Missouri. Hauled
by a handsomely groomed heavy 4-6-4, No. 173, the Nickel Plate Limited, running between Chicago and New York via Nickel Plate and Lackawanna, is shown
passing through South Gary, Indiana, on the eastbound run.

Lucius Beebe

ON THE SANTA FE TRAIL

The Chief, hauled by a Santa Fe Baldwin-built Northern-type 4-8-4, No. 3762, hits the California fruit country between Pasadena and San Bernardino.

ALONG THE MOBILE AND OHIO

There is about most Diesel-powered trains, no matter how luxurious, the disenchantment of a necessitous age, but this two-unit local running out of St. Louis terminal on the Mobile and Ohio's local run to Cairo and Jackson is possessed of a broad observation-platform on the second car, a traditional feature scorned by many modern train-designers.

Lucius Bee

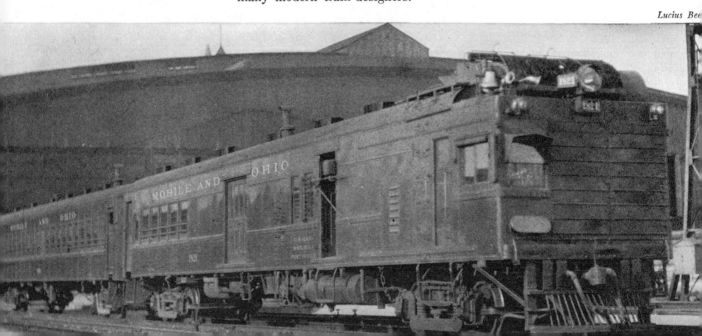

freight trains over the district between Mandan, North Dakota, and Glendive, Montana, where grades are long and severe. (On level ground the 2-8-8-4 can handle more than 15,000 tons.) One of the features of the engine was its enormous boiler and fire-box, the latter being about 9 feet wide and 22 feet long (with a grate area of 182 square feet)—big enough, the enginemen said, to hold the annual company picnic on.

While this 2-8-8-4 represents the peak of weight and power—a larger steam locomotive doubtless never will be constructed—and while it has generous proportions when compared to older Mallets, it can't be cited as an example of the most modern articulated engine. The trend to-day is to lighter locomotives, and to such wheel arrangement as the 4-6-6-4 and 2-6-6-4, with big driving-wheels, proportionately less weight on them, and ability to make steam when hauling a lighter train more swiftly. The 4-6-6-4s of the Northern Pacific and Union Pacific seem to be the coming thing; showing their greatest efficiency in speed ranges which were previously outside the abilities of articulated engines, they are employed not only for fast freight, but occasionally for main line passenger runs. Mutation, indeed, has manifested itself in locomotive design when an articulated engine is used for express passenger trains.

The Western Pacific has bought seven of the 4-6-6-4 arrangement, and the Denver and Rio Grande Western, ten; and the Pittsburgh and West Virginia, the Virginian, and Seaboard Air Line are using the 2-6-6-4 with marked success. The 2-6-6-4 is more distinctly a freight-hauler; but on the Seaboard Air Line, where it has 70-inch driving-wheels, it is said to wheel heavy passenger trains on occasion.

One of the most interesting cases of articulated engines in passenger service is to be found on the Southern Pacific, which now has 77 of the 4-8-8-2 type—in effect, the 2-8-8-4 type turned around and run fire-box first. This was done to increase the visibility of the engine crew in the snow-sheds and on curves; it is possible only because the engines burn oil, which is piped from the tender to the fire-box. If they burned coal the front end of the tender would have to be up against the cab. They are used in the Tehachapi Mountains, in helper service east of Los Angeles, and over the Sierras between Roseville, California, and Sparks, Nevada, where they handle both freight and passenger trains.

All these locomotives, from the 4-6-4 to the 4-6-6-4, are main line

Ivan Dmitr

engines. Unfortunately perhaps, the railroads have paid little attention to developing small machines in the modern style; apparently they feel the older main line engines are good enough, or that much of the branch line business isn't worth spending money on. With a half dozen exceptions, such as the Hiawatha 4-4-2s, the B. & O.'s 4-4-4, no steam locomotive has been constructed in the United States recently with the idea of providing power for swift, light passenger trains. In Canada, though, there seems to be revived hope for the building up of a profitable local service. The Canadian Pacific now has two dozen very light (120 to 135 tons) engines of the 4-4-4 type, which are easy on the track, capable of fast acceleration and very high speed, but suited for loads of no more than 300 or 350 tons under ordinary conditions. It would seem that

American railroads will have to consider something like this, for they can't assign to-day's enormous main line locomotives to lighter service when the present branch-line engines are done for.

While all this was happening to the steam locomotive, it was meeting very little competition from the electric engine, which was at one time expected to rule the rails by 1925. After the Milwaukee's expensive venture of 1915 and 1916, and the wave of terminal electrifications before the War, one big fact began to be appreciated: it cost almost as much to electrify a railroad as it did to construct a brand-new one. Since all such expenditures are made with borrowed money, and it is still considered good form to pay interest on borrowed money, the carrying charges of the projects probably exceeds the savings due to it.

In the case of the Pennsylvania, which now boasts more miles of electrified track than any other railroad, several things have made it justifiable if not staggeringly profitable. One is that part of its eastern lines was already electrified, and still more would have to be to carry the large volume of what amounts to commuting traffic, in which steam engines are both a nuisance to the unimaginative folk along the track and at a disadvantage in the matter of schedules. That meant almost all the line between New York City and Wilmington, Delaware. Since it was coming sooner or later, the Pennsy wired its entire line east of Harrisburg and northeast of Washington. This, it seems, will be the last big electrification project for a long time. Plainly, no road can afford to expend the price of a new railroad on such a project.

The operating advantages of electric locomotives, nowadays, are not so positive and so numerous as electrified railroads would have the public believe. While they can accelerate more swiftly under 30 miles an hour, they are not so lively in the higher speed ranges. One of the Pennsy's GG-1 engines can achieve 90 miles an hour with a 12-car train in six miles and six minutes after starting, but a properly designed steam-engine could hit 90 in half the time and distance, even though the electric is far ahead at 30 miles an hour. Theoretically, the electric has greater availability, but in practice the margin is not great. Steam locomotives are running up as many as 18,000 miles a month these days, and can't be compared unfavorably with competitors on this count. Electric locomotives are at least twice as expensive, and hence cost more to own. In fuel and other operating expenses, they no doubt have the edge; but against that edge must be balanced the initial and interest cost of electrification itself.

The most considerable rival of the steam locomotive is the Diesel-electric, which, though it looks to be of simple construction from the outside, is very complex internally, and by the same token more efficient thermally than a steam-engine, getting more than twice as much out of its fuel dollar. (It can go three times as far or haul three times the load, but it generally uses a better grade of oil, and thus can't convert the advantage into net advantage.) A Diesel-electric really consists of three engines: the Diesel engine itself, the generator, and the electric motors which are geared to the drivers, so it is expensive to build, costing at least four times as much as a steamer of the same capacity. Though it uses no water to speak of, and requires little to house and service, its repair and lubricating costs are high. All told, despite its greater thermal efficiency, there is every reason to believe it costs more than a steam locomotive, at least in road service, when all expenses are taken into consideration.

It does make a highly efficient switch engine, though, having been developed for yard service back in 1923, and used by many railroads ten years before anybody heard of the Diesel-electric streamliners. Its virtues as a switcher lie in the fact that it can be operated just about 24 hours a day, and that it boasts a very high starting tractive force. Not that it has more starting tractive force than the steamer of the same weight—for the tractive force of no locomotive can surpass by any considerable amount a quarter of the weight on its drivers—but that a Diesel-electric of a given horse-power has as much starting pull as a steamer of three times that horse-power—or, to put it another way, that the steamer develops more horse-power per ton of weight. What this works down to is that a Diesel-electric switcher can be purchased almost as cheaply as a steamer of the same starting tractive force, and that this fact, coupled with high availability, serves to cancel out expensive maintenance and give the Diesel switcher an advantage.

In road service this high starting tractive force is fully as much a disadvantage as an advantage. It makes for rapid acceleration in the lower speed ranges, but the pull falls off so abruptly that at 60 miles

an hour it does not equal the pull of a steam-engine with a third as much starting tractive force. So a Diesel-electric has to be enormously heavy to haul even a medium-sized train at 110 or 115 miles an hour. For a realistic comparison of the two, there may be offered the Santa Fe's new 4500-horse-power 4-6-4 type steam-engines against the 5400-horse-power Diesel-electrics which haul the City of San Francisco and City of Los Angeles. To begin with, the steamer costs $138,000, while the Diesel-electric came to $625,000. The steamer has only 49,300 pounds of starting tractive force, against more than 160,000 for the Diesel; but at 60 miles an hour the steamer has 21,300 pounds and at 80 miles an hour it has 13,700 pounds, against 19,000 and 10,700 for the Diesel. This, of course, means a livelier engine in the higher speed ranges, as well as the sheer power to haul more. The 4-6-4 weighs about 360 tons with its tender two-thirds full, while the Diesel comes to nearly 500 tons when the auxiliary motors are figured in. In general terms the steam locomotive is capable of higher speeds and it certainly can pull the same pay-load more swiftly or a greater load just as fast.

These circumstances do not make it probable that the Diesel motor will become the dominant motive power on American railroads in any very immediate future. What, then, are the advantages of the Diesel?

The most obvious is that of fuel consumption. A Diesel unit hauling an 8oo-ton train consumes only about two and a half gallons of fuel oil per mile against the nearly eight gallons required for the same performance by an oil-burning steam locomotive. That the quality of crude oil required for Diesel consumption is somewhat higher and hence a trifle more costly does not entirely cancel out the advantage of the Diesel's smaller consumption, although the interest charges, running from $100 a day up on the cost price of a Diesel unit may never be quite forgotten by the owning company. It will, too, be apparent that the cost of shopping a Diesel unit, reported to be an unfortunately frequent occurrence in their present state of development, is an added nightmare of expense on this basis alone.

Then there is the matter of water, and here it is that, especially in the western deserts and on long hauls through Utah, New Mexico and Arizona, the Diesel shines to best advantage. A Diesel needs neither a tank stop every 200 miles nor track pans for taking fuel water on the fly. This is obviously an urgent consideration where water is both scarce and bad. There are stretches of the Texas and Pacific where boiler water has been piped for distances of more than 200 miles and the chemical treatment of water found improper for boilers is no small consideration; neither is the necessity for keeping it above 32 degrees.

There are, too, considerations quite removed from the realm of the mechanical. They involve the popular imagination, which has been no negligible factor in the revival of rail passenger traffic in recent years and upon which a very considerable impression has been made by the high-pressure exploitation to which Diesel power has been subjected. And they involve the tremendous internal compulsion which makes vital for the automotive industry some further field of economic expansion.

That the comparative steam and Diesel operating costs and economies, have been often exaggerated, there can be no doubt.

Nothing in this summation calls for any moralization. That the public, through the certainly innocent device of "streamlining," has been induced to evince a reawakened interest in railroad travel and the legend and wonder of railroading calls for nothing but universal approval. That the merits of a new type of motive power are being exploited with the compulsive insistence which is the essence of the American system will comfort the cynical, and it may even be that, at some future date, the product will justify the premature claims made in its behalf.

The indications would seem that the race for supremacy between traditional steam motive power and the devisings of Diesel engineers will probably result in as great an improvement in the efficiency of railroad power during the next three decades as have characterized the last thirty transportation years. Spurred by the encroachments of Diesel, steam-engine builders will unquestionably still further improve upon the performances of their machinery. Plagued with the knowledge that their machine is theoretically and, perhaps, inherently more effective than steam, Diesel-electric engineers will strive to translate that margin of superiority into actual efficiency. The race, here as elsewhere, will belong to the strong.

Railroad Photographs

4   *DE LUXE*

WHEN the City of Los Angeles pulls out of the North Western terminal in Chicago on one of its five monthly sailings for the Pacific coast there is present all the *de luxe* circumstance of departure which accompanies a trans-Atlantic greyhound. Florists' boys deliver quantities of costly cut flowers; there is a crimson carpet a quarter of a mile long laid the length of the platform; trucks of luggage bearing the hall-marks of celebrated foreign makers and the labels of the world's luxury hotels discharge their cargoes at the baggage-car; and the scene is pervaded by an atmosphere of opulence more often associated with foreign voyaging than domestic travel.

Nor does the illusion vanish aboard the fourteen sleek yellow and brown seamlessly welded passenger-cars of the seventeen-car streamliner where pastel shades, severe paneling and chromium trim have replaced the plush, hassocks, *cloisonné* and elaborate crystal bewilderment which gave to an entire era of national taste the name of Pullman. Morning-coated *maîtres d'hôtel*, who might have stepped from the restaurants of fashion in any world center, respectfully await the commands of diners in a restaurant-car which dwarfs all previous conceptions of railroad train spaciousness. Handsomely chaste menus the size of sheet music list a simple but catholic selection of dishes quite different from the profusion of ornate *entrées* of the bills of fare of yesterday. There is a noble wine list. There are automatic telephones, barbers, valets and maids, stewards, bartenders and porters. There are cut flowers, state-rooms big enough to be decorated with movable furniture, there is the Little Nugget, a bar-car recreating the frontier atmosphere of bonanza days, there are air-conditioning, individual state-room heat and humidity controls, there are indirect lighting, wide expanses of window for every seat and cars for coach passengers characterized by refinement of decoration and comfort undreamed of half a decade ago. Dustless, noiseless, vibrationless, the City of Los Angeles with 254 passengers peopling its lounges and restaurant, drawing-rooms, sections

163

and coaches, flashes across the miles from Chicago to the Pacific in fewer than forty hours, a rolling microcosm of all the world's luxuries.

It required a time investment of eleven railroading decades or nearly four generations of American life to evolve the Chicago and North Western–Union Pacific's most magnificent train and the many comparable passenger flyers that have been designed in recent times. Certainly to-day's streamliners and the more traditional crack limiteds with standard equipment and steam power are amazing in contrast with the austere simplicity of the first trains of a hundred years ago, but the impulse toward luxurious rail travel is as old as successful railway operation itself. Some of the manifestations of this urge are to-day provocative of amused superiority; almost all of them have about them the wistful quality of only yesterday's antiquity. The antimacassar, the looped and frilled curtain, the plush and ormolu and marquetry of Victorian times may be humorously ornate, but they are also souvenirs of the golden age of America and of securities, integrities and emotions vanished and never to be recaptured.

Probably the first luxury train ever operated in the United States is chronicled in the journal of a traveler of the early forties on the rails of the Auburn and Rochester Railroad.

The cars are twenty-eight feet long and eight feet wide [he wrote of this paragon of magnificence]. The seats are well stuffed and admirably arranged with arms for each chair and changeable backs so that passengers may change from front to rear by a manoeuvre unknown in military tactics. The size of the car forms a pleasant room, handsomely painted, with floor matting, with windows secured from jarring and with curtains to shield from the blazing sun. We should have said rooms, for there is in each car a ladies' apartment with luxurious sofas and seats, and in recesses may be found a washstand and other conveniences.... The ladies can now have their choice of a sofa in their own apartment or a seat in the main saloon of the cars as their health and inclination may require. These cars are hung on springs, and of such large size that they are free from most of the jar, and especially the swinging motion so disagreeable to most railroads.

Another extra-magnificent train which popped the eyes and roused the imaginations of the citizenry of the stovepipe hat and hoop-skirt

decade was the Boston and Albany's special, a veritable miracle of elegance, which brought the Prince of Wales from Albany to Boston in the year 1860. The Prince himself confessed he was impressed by "the conveniences of the toilette which furnished running water from a mysterious source," by the several saloon-cars fairly awash with Turkey carpets, bronze cuspidors, inlaid woodwork, stained glass, *cloisonné*, gilt French clocks and "solid silver drinking accommodations tastefully set forth upon marquetry tables."

Something of the informal charm of rail travel at a still earlier date when railroading was conducted with all the casual abandon of present day motor traffic was described in 1846 by Hasket Derby, a New Englander of local note in his generation.

That long array of cars, laden with stone, onions and fish, ice, slippers and bricks, interspersed with passengers, moving in slow procession on their winding way to Boston. They stop at Danvers for the onions; near the Salem pastures to collect the boulders; at Brown's pond for the ice; at Gravesend for the fish; at the Print Works for the slippers; and opposite Breed's Hotel [then a well-known drinking place in Lynn] to receive the inanimate and moisten the animate clay. I will leave our friends at this exciting spot and take passage in the regular train of the Eastern Railroad, which whistles by like a rocket on the air line to Boston.

Ten years after the Prince's polite amazement another veritable cyclone of excitement was caused throughout the country by the passage, in the first year of its completion and over the new Pacific Railroad, of a train that was a miracle of contemporary elegance and a wonderment all the way from Boston to San Francisco.

With rails for the first time stretching—with the sole exception of the breadth of the Missouri River at Omaha—from Park Square to the water's edge of Oakland, the members of the Boston Board of Trade organized for themselves and their families an elaborate overland junket and went to call on the first citizens of St. Francis' town. The trip west occupied from May 24 to May 31, 1870, including a stop-over but no change of cars at Chicago, wherein the traveling public of last century seemed better served than it has ever been since, when through trains from the Atlantic seaboard to the Pacific are unknown and every one must ferry himself and his possessions from one depot to another in the Windy City.

The train followed the right of way of the Boston and Albany to Albany, the New York Central to Niagara Falls, to Detroit by the Great Western of Canada, via Michigan Central to Chicago and thence west over the familiar route of the Chicago and North Western, Union Pacific and Central Pacific. Not the least of its modern improvements was a printing-press in the smoking-car wherefrom a daily newspaper was issued throughout the trip with the following description in its columns of the train's own and many distinguishing features.

The train [said *The Transcontinental*] is made up of eight of the most elegant cars ever drawn over an American railway. They were built by order of the Messrs. Pullman, to be completed in time for the present excursion, and to be first used in conveying the members of the Board of Trade of the city of Boston, and their families, from their homes on the Atlantic coast to the shores of the Pacific.

The train leads off with a baggage car, the front of which has five large ice closets, and a refrigerator, for the storing of fruits, meat and vegetables. The balance of the car is for baggage, with the exception of a square in one corner, where stands a new quarto-medium Gordon press, upon which this paper is printed.

Next comes a very handsome smoking car, which is divided into four rooms. The first is the printing office, which is supplied with black walnut cabinets filled with the latest styles of type for newspaper and job work. This department, we may say without egotism, has been thoroughly tested, and has already turned out some as fine work as can be done by those of our brothers who have a local habitation. Adjoining this is a neatly fitted up lobby and wine room. Next comes a large smoking room, with euchre tables, etc. The rear end of the car has a beautifully furnished hair-dressing and shaving saloon.

Following this come the two new hotel cars, the "Arlington" and the "Revere," both of which are completely and elegantly furnished, and are thoroughly adapted to the uses for which they are destined. Two magnificent saloon cars, the "Palmyra" and "Marquette" come next. The train is completed by the two elegant commissary cars, the "St. Charles" and "St. Cloud," each of which is finished in all of its appointments as any of the other carriages noticed.

The entire train is equipped with every desirable accessory that may tend in the least to promote the ease of the passengers—elaborate hangings, costly upholstery, artistic gilding, and beautifully finished wood work marking every portion of their arrangements. Among the new features introduced into these cars are two well-stocked libraries, replete with choice works of fiction, history, poetry, etc., and two of the improved Burdett organs. These instruments are complete in every detail of stops, pedals, double banks of keys, etc.

The cars of this train are lighted during the night in a new and novel manner, there being under each an ingeniously constructed machine which produces from liquid hydro-carbon, a gas equal in brilliancy to that made in the ordinary way....

The menus on the "hotel" cars and diners which began to appear on the crack trains of the later sixties specialized in a vast profusion of

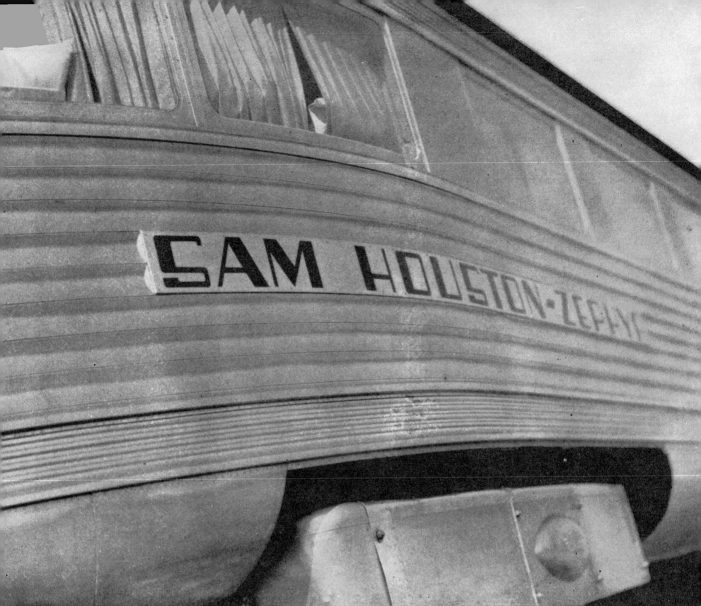

Lucius Be

soups and fish courses, *entrées,* games, roasts and sweets which are unfamiliar in a day when economy of space prohibits their wide variety. The bill of fare on the Pullman hotel-car "President" which was put into service on the Great Western Railroad (now the Grand Trunk) in 1867 listed oysters raw, fried, roasted, *soufflé* and *en brochette.* There were grouse and partridge, pheasant, woodcock, heath-hen, quail, antelope meat, venison, roast beef, mutton and fowl, golden plover, blue-winged teal, canvasback, veal cutlets, snipe and Kansas City steaks of heroic proportions for sixty cents. Rum omelette was half a dollar. Hock and claret, Burgundy and Champagne, Pisco brandy and Medford rum all flowed in amiable Niagaras.

The substantial citizenry tucked their napkins in their collars, took a firm grip on their eating tools and put away everything on the bill from sardines and terrapin stew right through to Indian pudding with hard sauce. The dining-car glories of the era so impressed an editorial writer on the staff of the New York *Tribune* that he even ventured to forecast the day when trains might boast a barber shop as well as *de luxe* restaurant service. "This too may come," he told the pop-eyed readers of Mr. Greeley's paper, "as last summer an excursion party of ladies and gentlemen took a hair dresser with them over the Erie to Niagara Falls, and two or three of the ladies actually had their hair crimped while traveling thirty or forty miles an hour."

Before the New York, New Haven and Hartford was looted by the elder Morgan it was one of the most prosperous and conservative railroad properties in the world. Hardly an estate in New England but listed at least a few shares, and a passed dividend was unheard-of. The agricultural and manufactured products of New England were freighted on what amounted to a railroad monopoly to the South and West, and the affairs of the company were handled in a manner that was the quintessence of competent conservatism.

The New England Limited was the crack passenger train of the combined New York and New England and New Haven roads. It first went into service in November, 1884, but it was not until March, 1891, that it appeared resplendent in the gold-leaf and varnish that was to make the White Train the pride of New England and almost as much of a legend as the Union Pacific's Overland Flyer which had been put in service two years before and was astounding the West with its speed and luxury.

Its sections left the Grand Central Terminal on the leased tracks of the New York Central, and on the tracks of the New York and New England from that road's depot at the foot of Summer Street at 3 o'clock every afternoon and made the run between New York and Boston in an even six hours. The New Haven's crack daylight trains, the Yankee Clipper and the Merchants' Limited, were later to make the Boston–New York run over the Shore Line in four and a half hours, but six was the last word in speed in the nineties.

Seven cars, all painted cream-white and hauled by a beautiful, high-stepping eight-wheeler, were peopled with Lowells and Hallowells, Lodges and Saltonstalls, who bowed to each other with expressions of outrageous satisfaction amidst the bristling thickets of mirrors, potted palms and scrolled baggage-racks which illustrated its positively Byzantine lounges.

The parlor cars are furnished with velvet carpets [reported a breathless contemporary], as well as with silk draperies and white silk curtains; the chairs are upholstered in old gold plush and large wall mirrors set off the cars handsomely.... The Royal Buffet smokers which will be run in addition to the ordinary smoking cars are decorated in the same manner as the parlor cars and contain twenty-four handsomely upholstered chairs for parlor car passengers. The Pullman Palace Car Company has designed a special dining car for the train.

Railroad travelers to-day find their surroundings aboard the crack luxury flyers of the land characterized by less gaudy magnificence. The decorative schemes of the newest *de luxe* limiteds run to the chaste simplicities of subdued modernism with straight lines, wide expanses of window, indirect lighting, chromium trim and severe pine paneling. There has been a vast increase in the number of private compartments, drawing-rooms and *en suite* living quarters both in Pullmans and in cars built by individual railroads and the single sleeping-room cars which are standard equipment on almost all overnight hauls, such as those of the Twentieth Century Limited, the Broadway and the Wolverine between New York and Chicago, the New Haven's Owl and the Washington sleeping trains of the Pennsylvania, are usually sold out before the supply of lowers and sections has been exhausted. Probably the handsomest train compartments in the world are those of the Super Chief and the City of Los Angeles, while on the Forty-niner and several other trains the Pullman Company has been experimenting with double-deck single-room cars. The principle deficiency in the design of these has been their small window-space and absence of storage room for luggage.

Sadly enough and to the vexation of a very considerable number of

MOUNTAIN DIVISION

With valves popping and smoke exhausts rolling up the mountainside, five locomotives thunder up the 3 per cent grade of Soldier Summit, Utah, with eleven
mail and Pullman cars of the Denver and Rio Grande Train No. 6. Here is the
archetypal action shot of railroading in the old West.

Courtesy of the Atchison, Topeka and Santa F

NAVAJO MOTIF

Aboard the Santa Fe's Super Chief the decorative scheme is suggestive of the southwestern country-side through which the train passes on the Chicago–Los Angeles run and the observation-lounge is patterned in Navajo colors and figures.

CENTRAL PACIFIC, 1869

This is the Pullman Palace Commissary-Car "Wotkins," of the type used on transcontinental trains shortly after the Central Pacific–Union Pacific line was opened in 1869. These were the first diners and were operated only on what were known as *de luxe* "Hotel Trains," usually consisting of three Pullman Palace parlor-sleeping cars, the commissary-car, four Silver Palace sleeping-cars belonging to the Central Pacific, two ordinary coaches and a baggage-car, making an 11-car train. There was a $10 extra fare for riding on the Pullman cars and passengers who did not want to pay the extra fare ate at railroad eating-houses.

Upper right: Co
of the Southern Pa

LUXURY TRAVEL IN CIVIL WAR DAYS

Ablaze with varnish and gilt and elaborately decorated with tassels and brocade this drawing-room coach, the Garden City, was the pride of the Lake Shore and Michigan Southern Railroad, now a part of the New York Central.

Lower right: Cou
of the Southern P

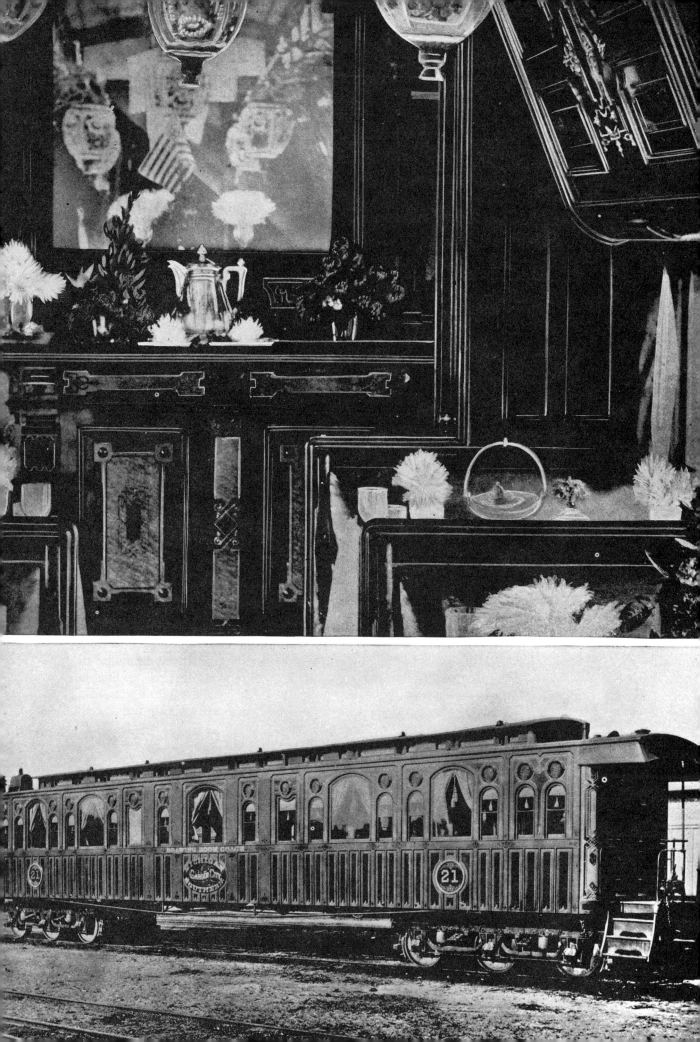

Lucius Be

THE GLORY OF THE FRISCO

The St. Louis–San Francisco Railroad has about it an atmosphere of wonder and romance that has eluded greater and more far-reaching transcontinental lines. Its 5,300 miles of rails span Missouri and Kansas, Oklahoma, Arkansas and Mississippi and extend into Texas and Alabama. It builds some of its own motive power at its Springfield, Missouri, shops. Its freight is the incalculably rich produce of all the deep southwest, and its varnish trains are sleek and beautiful in the old manner, green and gold and flashing across the country-side to the drum-fire of engine exhausts. Here is the Bluebonnet at Webster Grove, Missouri, hitting 70 as the driver gets into his stride on the St. Louis–Dallas–Fort Worth run. The Frisco's 4-8-2, No. 1509, gleams with a brass bell, polished cylinder heads and red and gold markers.

Lucius Beebe

IRON HORSE, STEEL ALLOY HARNESS

In common with the Southern Pacific's Daylight, the New York Central's Mercury and the Texas and New Orleans (Southern Pacific's) Sunbeams, the Reading Lines' new passenger streamliner Crusader on the New York–Philadelphia run is powered with standard steam equipment housed in a stainless steel shroud, hauling light-weight passenger-coaches. For this purpose the Reading turned over to the Edward G. Budd Manufacturing Company a conventional Reading Pacific-type steam locomotive, precisely similar to the one shown hauling the Seven O'Klocker, which was rebuilt as is shown in another photograph. It is shown hitting nearly 80 miles an hour on the eastbound run on a winter dawn near Plainfield, New Jersey. Below is one of the Texas and New Orleans (Southern Pacific) Sunbeams, built from a reconditioned 1913 model Pacific, on the Houston run just south of Dallas.

Lucius Beebe

DE LUXE ON THE CHESAPEAKE AND OHIO

The Chesapeake and Ohio's Train No. 5-47, the Sportsman, heads into Alexandria, Virginia, behind one of the road's gleaming Super-Pacifics on the Cincinnati-Chicago run. The Sportsman is a solid steel, air-conditioned varnish train, a companion to the George Washington and the Fast Flying Virginian, and in this photograph, taken just south of the long bridge over the Potomac, it comprises twelve cars and a locomotive equipped with a Super-Vanderbilt tender.

BEDTIME ON THE N.Y.C.

It is possible that the artist exaggerates the spacious proportions of this Wagner Sleeping Car, especially in the width of the aisle, but otherwise it would seem a faithful version of night-life aboard one of the "elegantly appointed" through trains of the Central in the seventies. The wood-burning stove, which so frequently made holocaust consequent upon train wreck at this period, looms in the foreground. Lighting was by hydrocarbon gas and berths were in triple decks. Aware of the Victorian proprieties, all the gentlemen are depicted as retiring wearing stocks around their necks.

PLOVER'S EGGS AND CLARET

The Union Pacific diner of the year 1870 was a more robust restaurant than are the snack-cars of to-day. While the Mormon behind him peruses Mr. Greeley's New York *Tribune*, the gentleman front and right refreshes himself with a half bottle of Perriet Jouet, English *cuvée*. The vintage of '64 was highly esteemed at the time.

PRIDE OF THE MONON

Every morning a few moments before noon, when the Santa Fe's *de luxe* Chief pulls out of the Dearborn Station in Chicago for its run to the coast, three somewhat less celebrated but none-the-less handsome little varnish trains are high-balled out into the main on their daylight runs to distant cities. They are the Banner Blue of the Wabash, the Chicago, Indianapolis and Louisville's Tippecanoe and the St. Louis Zipper of the Chicago and Eastern Illinois. Each of them partakes of the old-time tradition of immaculate power and equipment and from pilot to observation platform they gleam like yachts. Here is the Monon's Tippecanoe, southbound and gathering speed as she heads out of Cedar Lake, Illinois, for Indianapolis, by way of Monon, Indiana.

MAIN LINE SOUTHWEST

Behind an imposing 4-8-2 the Missouri Pacific's Sunshine Special, first section of two daily, rolls impressively out of St. Louis on the run which includes Fort Worth, Houston, New Orleans and San Antonio. The Sunshine is the Mop's crack luxury train and runs with standard equipment including an observation-lounge decorated in Mission style with adobe-finished walls and wrought-iron grille-work partitions.

THE PRIDE OF THE TEXAS AND PACIFIC

Hitting around 70 miles an hour in the face of the setting sun just east of Abilene, Texas, the California and West Texas Section of the Sunshine Special heads for El Paso where its Pullmans will meet the rails of the Southern Pacific for the desert haul to Southern California. It is powered by a recently shopped Pacific, No. 718, whose cylinder heads, brasswork and rod assembly gleam gold and silver in the old railroading tradition as it flashes over the Lone Star miles.

THE GOLDEN STATE

Over the iron of the Rock Island Lines from Chicago to Tucumcari, New Mexico, where it meets the Southern Pacific, the Golden State Limited is one of the most handsomely appointed of the great transcontinental trains daily out of Chicago for the Pacific coast. A luxury train without extra service charges, the Golden State is the ranking varnish of the Rock Island's 8,000 miles of rails. The line's other crack train is the Rocky Mountain Limited on the Chicago-Denver run. Hauled by a Mountain-type locomotive, No. 4015, and trailing fifteen mail-cars and Pullmans, the Golden State is shown heading out of Englewood, Illinois.

THE KATY FLYER

Heading out of Fort Worth on the Kansas City–St. Louis run, the Missouri–Kansas-Texas Lines' No. 6-26 gathers speed behind a ten-wheeler of venerable design. Starting from San Antonio, the Katy Flyer picks up and sets out sleeping-cars through half the southwest, pulling into St. Louis with the sunrise with a leash of fourteen or fifteen mail and Pullman cars.

YARD GOAT DE LUXE

Probably the most exquisitely tended switching engine in the world is this aristo-crat among yard goats which reshuffles varnish trains on the Southern Pacific tracks at Sacramento. Cylinder heads, bell, whistle, number plate, headlight case, injectors and all the boiler mountings in the cab are nickel-plated. Other parts are painted in silver, and tires, motion, reverse gear, hand-rails and such are burnished like mirrors.

ALMOST TO TIMBER-LINE

No railroad is freighted with more romantic appeal than the Denver and Rio Grande Western whose iron brackets the Rockies with two routes between the Colorado capital and the Great Salt Lake of Utah. Over the grades of the old Salt Lake and Denver City by way of the Moffat Tunnel No. 5, the Panoramic, is a crack mountain division passenger haul, famous for its fresh mountain trout, its overnight convenience and its breathless heights.

AMIDST THE "ROARING TOWNS"

Through Elko, Carlin, Palisade and Beowawe in wildest Nevada runs the iron of the Western Pacific, double-tracking with the Southern Pacific from Alazon to Winnemucca to secure grade advantage. From Salt Lake City to San Francisco through Feather River Canyon where the winter snows pile up to a depth of 40 feet the Western Pacific is the Espee's only rival as an important transcontinental freight and passenger road. Dominant in the road's finances and chairman of its board for many years has been bearded, seagoing Arthur Curtiss James of New York. The Western Pacific's crack passenger train, No. 1, the Scenic Limited, hauled by 4-8-4 No. 175, is shown pulling out of Elko on the westbound run which will find it at Oakland Pier the next morning.

ORANGE AND RED AND BLACK: THE DAYLIGHT

A million-dollar flyer, the Southern Pacific's Daylight on the Los Angeles–San Francisco run is probably the most spectacular train ever designed. A streamlined, air-conditioned steam train built of stainless steel and brilliantly lacquered in orange, red and black, this express is drawn by a 4-8-4 fitted with disk drivers and an enlarged tender over the *Camino Real,* the King's Highway, that once linked the Spanish missions of California, embracing practically every type of country known to railroading from the Santa Clara Valley, over the rough Santa Lucia Mountains and along the cliffs of the Pacific Ocean for more than a hundred breathless miles. The locomotives were built by Lima at a cost of $140,000 each and there are twelve cars to each train equipped with every convenience and luxury known to modern speed transportation. A campaign of advertising throughout the nation when the Daylight's run was inaugurated made it one of the best paying passenger hauls on the Espee's sailing list.

WHEN ALL THE WORLD WAS YOUNG

The New England Limited shown as it took on water at the track pans installed for its service at Putnam, Connecticut, in the autumn of 1891. This luxury flyer, better known to the nineties as the White Train, made the Boston to New York run in an atmosphere of cream and gold cars, plush upholstery and handsome bronze cuspidors which left travelers breathless in the mustache-cup and livery-stable era. It was jointly owned by the New York and New England and the New York, New Haven and Hartford and made the daily run in the amazing time of six hours over the route through inland Connecticut known as the Air Line. This photograph, one of the rarest of collector's items, was taken just at sundown and is remarkable for its clarity of detail and action at a time when action photographs were extremely uncommon.

All photographs courtesy of the New York, New Haven and Hartford

THE PRIDE OF THE NEW YORK
AND NEW ENGLAND

Throughout the eighties the New England Limited was painted a conventional black, but in the spring of 1891 it dazzled all beholders by streaking across the Connecticut country-side in cream and gold tints. Before the day of the New Haven's celebrated Knickerbocker and Merchants' Limited she was the wonder and glory of the Boston–New York run and, at what was literally the end of the century, she was a very *fin de siècle* train indeed.

THE GLORY THAT WAS THE WHITE TRAIN

The restaurant-car of the White Train was the last word in *chic* in the nineties. The carpet was Turkey red, after sundown it was illuminated by Pintsch lights, the walls were covered with a basket fabric in subdued shades and the tables were separated one from another by heavy brocaded curtains so that privacy might be assured the elderly and genteel ladies of the time who were not quite sure either that the railroads were here to stay or that it was entirely refined to dine in public.

TASSELS, HASSOCKS AND PLUSH

The work of the Pullman Palace Car Company. There were seven parlor-cars such as this in the two daily sections of the White Train as well as two Royal Buffet-Smokers, four coaches and two restaurant-cars. Plate-glass mirrors, silk draperies and looped silk curtains, not to omit the plush chairs, each with its attendant hassock, achieved a new high in modish elegance. Even maiden ladies from Beacon Street going over to New York to stop at the Murray Hill Hotel agreed that the White Train was entirely respectable.

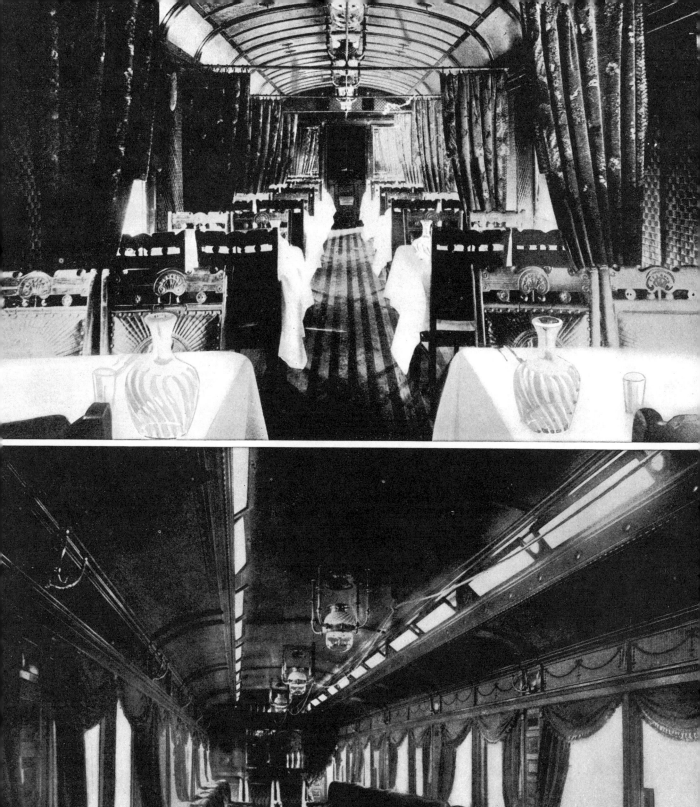

travelers, the brass-railed observation-platform, so long a characteristic and American institution, is giving way to inclosed cars with glassed-in lounges. Why this innovation should be evolved coincidentally with the perfecting of Diesel power, which eliminates soot and cinders, is one of the fatuous features of what passes for "progress." The dynamic value of streamed and teardrop and beavertail car-ends is, of course, simply non-extant for practical consideration.

Perhaps the most fascinating aspect of rail travel has always been the business of dining *en route*. Voyagers of only a few years ago were familiar with the now almost obsolete institution of the twenty-minute meal stop at station restaurants situated advantageously along the line and their excellence or the reverse, the charms of their waitresses and the potency of the native spirits became part of the traveling man's legend. To-day the dining-car is universal and it exists in a score or more of variations which include lounge-diners, buffets, club restaurants, cafeteria-cars, breakfast counters, stand-up bars and *de luxe* restaurant-cars with frock-coated *maîtres d'hôtel* and stainless steel eating tools.

When the French Count Boni de Castellane visited the United States to sue for the hand of Anna Gould he recorded in his diary that all the guests aboard Jay Gould's private train were accustomed to appear for dinner in formal evening-dress and that the private apartments of the travelers swarmed with butlers and valets, footmen, lady's-maids and grooms of the chambers. Dressing for dinner is not, as it is with ocean voyagers, a general practice, but many restaurant-cars are as handsome in their appointments as Ritz restaurants and the cuisine of some is celebrated.

The New York Central's diners on the Chicago and St. Louis runs to New York are famed for the excellence of their Lake Erie whitefish, a delicacy rarely encountered save in the Great Lakes region. Fresh figs of monstrous proportions are served with thick cream as a specialty on the breakfast menus of the Southern Pacific. The Pennsylvania's salad bowl has become part of the national consciousness, and the browned rib-ends of beef on the New Haven are known to thousands.

Bar accommodations have received the attentions of such recognized designers as Henry Dreyfuss and Raymond Loewy, and amateurs of period design as well as Scotch are enchanted by the Little Nugget Bar of the City of Los Angeles which faithfully recreates, through the agency of *Police Gazette* illustrations, red-fringed table-cloths and a genuine stuffed canary in a gold cage, the atmosphere of a sample room of bonanza days. The lounge of the Pennsylvania's new Broadway Limited is finished in pastel shades of green and pale brown and aboard the Burlington's Denver Zephyr the passenger has a choice of three refreshment oases, the Pullman lounge, the restaurant-car and the stand-up bar in the coach-smoker forward. A part of the equipment of the Milwaukee Hiawatha, on the Chicago–Twin Cities run, is an air-conditioned, windowless and soundless tap-room, the windows having been eliminated lest the vision of the speeding country-side should alarm the more timid tipplers. Aboard the U.P.'s City of Denver there is the Frontier Shack, patterned, like the Little Nugget, along lines of pioneer taste, its walls illustrated with ancient playbills, wanted-for-murder posters, Remington rifles, prospectors' claims and other memorabilia of a more irrepressible and youthful Colorado.

The Florida Special, which transports winter vacationists over the rails of the Pennsylvania, Atlantic Coast Line, Florida East Coast and Richmond, Fredericksburg and Potomac, includes in its equipment a recreation car with pretty hostesses and a four-piece Hawaiian orchestra. The restaurant-cars of the New Haven's Yankee Clipper and Merchants' Limited, perhaps the most magnificently appointed standard construction daylight trains in the land, are in joint care of a morning-coated steward and a professional hostess, and their wine list, selected by Boston's celebrated grocery firm of S. S. Pierce and Company, fairly bristles with vintage *cuvées* and costly bonded spirits. The menus of the City of Los Angeles and Forty-niner list such luxuries as caviar, pheasant and green turtle on the fixed price meals, while such once undreamed-of conveniences as train secretaries, shower-baths, terminal telephone connections and stock-market reports are almost universally taken for granted.

The tale of the luxury trains of the land is far too long a one categorically to be recorded. In general they fall into two classifications: daylight runs on comparatively short hauls such as the Pennsylvania's Congressional Limited, the Southern Pacific's Daylight, the Boston and

DOWN EAST VARNISH

Hauled by Hudson No. 702 on her maiden trip, the Boston and Maine–Maine Central's crack daily passenger train between Boston, Portland and Bangor, the Flying Yankee, is shown hitting 70 miles an hour at Northern Maine Junction, Maine, with a haul of nine mail, coach and Pullman cars. The name Flying Yankee was later given to the streamlined Diesel train on the same run and the standard equipment express became known as the Pine Tree Limited.

THE FORTY-NINER COMES HOME

Upper right:
Lucius Beebe

Dusty from the deserts of Utah and Wyoming, the Forty-niner, streamlined, light-weight luxury train on the Chicago–San Francisco run over the rails of the Chicago and North Western, the Union and Southern Pacific, comes into the North Western yards at Chicago behind a speedy heavy Pacific. Powered by steam on all three roads, the Forty-niner boasts a streamlined locomotive to match its gray and gold *décor* on the Union Pacific run from Omaha to Ogden, and on the Espee's iron is hauled by a variety of power including a cab-first Mallet.

TWENTIETH CENTURY LIMITED, OLD STYLE

Lower right:
Lucius Beebe

The most famous train in the world and the standard of long-distance, high-speed operation for American railroad practice, the Century has captured the public imagination as no other limited has ever done. For more than three decades the New York Central's pride has covered the third of the continent between New York and Chicago on various schedules, the most recent of which is 16 hours.

"THE TALL FAR-TRAFFICKING SHAPES"

This high-stepping ten-wheeler of the Texas and Pacific is heading out of the Fort Worth terminal with the Louisiana Limited northbound of a May afternoon. Note the diminutive awning over the cab window on the fireman's side, a homely touch affected on most roads in Texas and the southwest where the sun is hot the year round.

Photographs courtesy of the New York Central

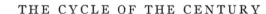

THE CYCLE OF THE CENTURY

Designed by Henry Dreyfuss and distinguished by a number of innovations both in motive power and in passenger accommodations, the New York Central's Twentieth Century Limited is an example of modern theories of design and streamlining combined with standard steam power. The Hudson-type locomotive, the outstanding passenger power where level tracks and low grades prevail as they do on the Central's New York–Chicago run, is capable of developing more than 4700 horse-power at 75 miles an hour and at 80 miles an hour has a draw-bar pull of 17,500 pounds. The reduced weight of drive-wheels and rod assemblies through the agency of light-weight steel mounted on roller-bearings has reduced dynamic augment, or the pound of revolving and reciprocating parts on the rails, more than 50 per cent. The locomotive is equipped with automatic stoker, power reverse gear, feed water-heater, rubber draft gear and a covered tender. The semi-circular fin on the boiler head serves both as ornament and as part of the smoke-deflector arrangement visible on the boiler top. Below is a corner of one of the two diners which are part of each train. In the late evening these luxury restaurants serve as cafés and night clubs.

Lucius Beeb

WABASH VARNISH

Famed as the source and training-school of many great railroaders, the Wabash is one of the roads to which, as to the Frisco and Denver and Rio Grande Western, there clings an indefinable flavor of romance. Above is No. 2, the Detroit and Toledo Special, pulling into the sunset in the St. Louis yards before heading eastward over the Merchants' Bridge. Although no stranger to financial difficulties, the Wabash boasts fine equipment and some of the most perfect stretches of road-bed in the land. Its Chicago–St. Louis run through the corn-fields and farm lands of Illinois is one of the most lyric of rail trips.

DEVISING OF LUXURIOUS MODERNITY

In the bar-lounge car of the Pennsylvania's 1938 edition of the Broadway Limited, styled and designed by Raymond Loewy and executed by the road's engineers at Altoona, rare woods, handsomely executed panels, mirrors, Venetian blinds and harmonious color schemes blend in simple good taste. The lighting is indirect, the colors themselves are variants and related shades of the Pennsylvania's traditional Tuscan-red: sand, brown, yellow and white. A circular bar serves the standing thirsty and there are service bars in the observation-lounge and restaurant-cars. Specially fabricated glass, silver and linen are part of the Broadway's luxurious equipment on its 16-hour run between New York and Chicago over the Pennsylvania mountains. Above is shown the Broadway drawn by a G. G. 1 electric between Paoli and Harrisburg.

Courtesy of the Pennsylvania

All photographs by Lucius Beebe

POWER ON THE NEW HAVEN

This is one of the New Haven's 1300 series of Pacifics which for many years have drawn such well-known trains on the New York–Boston run as the Merchants' Limited, Yankee Clipper, Senator, Knickerbocker and Colonial. On the New Haven's heavier trains the Pacific series is being supplanted by a fleet of ten new streamlined Hudsons, known to the New Haven as "Shoreliners," built for the road by Baldwin in 1937 and costing $110,000 each.

THE CITY OF DENVER

The Chicago and North Western–Union Pacific Diesel-powered streamliner City of Denver, overnight from Chicago, rolls past a grain-elevator and into the terminal yards in the Colorado capital. Featuring the most luxurious of accommodations for both coach and Pullman passengers and famous for the atmosphere of its Frontier Bar, the City of Denver is one of the world's fastest long-run trains and streaks across Illinois, Iowa and Nebraska to Denver, a distance of 1,047 miles between 6:20 P.M. in the evening and 9:20 A.M. the next morning.

IN THE OLD TRADITION

This brave little varnish is the Chicago and Eastern Illinois St. Louis Zipper setting out on its daily noontime run from Chicago to the Missouri metropolis. Handsomely appointed from pilot to gleaming observation rail, it rolls a coach, a diner and a Pullman lounge behind an immaculate light Pacific with an air and style no streamliner, however luxurious, can achieve.

Railroad Photographs

ON THE SHORE LINE

The New York, New Haven and Hartford's Yankee
Clipper, all-Pullman extra-fare limited on the
Boston–New York run, familiarly known to Bos-
tonians as "the One O'Clock," southbound near
Stonington, Connecticut. Perhaps the most quietly
affluent and cultivated passenger lists in America are
those on the New Haven's Yankee Clipper and
Merchants' Limited. On the Clipper the Pullmans
are named for celebrated New England merchant-
men of a century ago: Flying Cloud, Gamecock,
Nantucket Light.

MAPLE AND MARBLE ELEGANCE

This coach, the pride of the Eureka and Nevada in
days gone by, boasted Venetian blinds, birds'-eye
maple trim, solid brass fixtures and plumbing inci-
dentals and a marble basin in the washroom. When
precious metal was flowing from every mine shaft
in the western land and in nearby Colorado the Central City Opera House was jammed with booted
miners and gamblers fairly sagging with Colt's Frontier Model .45's to see Modjeska or Keene, nothing
was too good for the times.

Courtesy of A. Sheldon Pennoyer

Courtesy of Railroad Magazine

FIN DE SIECLE

This is the observation lounge-car on one of the Northern Pacific Railroad's limiteds at the turn of the century. Pintsch burners had given way to floriated
electroliers, electric fans presaged air-conditioning, but the fringed curtain, the
potted plant (on the extreme left) and the velvet table-cover still survived as
vestigial traces of an earlier Victorian scheme of decoration.

Courtesy of the Union Pacific

THE CITY OF LOS ANGELES

Capable of cruising speeds in excess of 110 miles an hour, almost a quarter of a mile long and certainly the last word in modern *de luxe* rail transport, the Union Pacific–Chicago and North Western's jointly owned City of Los Angeles runs on a 39¾-hour schedule between Chicago and the coast in direct competition with the Santa Fe's Super Chief. Its Diesel engines are synchronized to deliver 5400 horse-power. The City of Los Angeles' passenger quarters provide every type of train accommodation used in standard service; it has two intercommunicating telephone services, hot and cold water under air-pressure and the most elaborate eating and refreshment arrangements of any train in the world.

Courtesy of Railroad Magazine

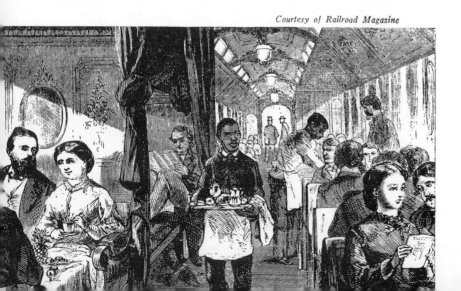

BEFORE THE STREAMLINERS

Here is a scene on a Union Pacific diner in the era of Macassar hair oil, Gladstone bags, and white beaver hats when *cabinets particuliers* were provided for luxury travelers.

CITY OF MEXICO

The weekly tourist special, which the Missouri Pacific runs out of St. Louis for the Mexican capital, in the St. Louis yards just east of Tower Grove. The City of Mexico, on a 47½-hour schedule, has in its consist *de luxe* sleepers and compartment-cars, lounge-bar, showers and other luxury equipment, and runs on the Mexican National south of Nuevo Loredo.

THE EMPIRE BUILDER, 1910

Courtesy of the Atchison, Topeka and Santa Fe

THE FIRST SUPER CHIEF

The first experimental Diesel-powered Super
Chief before the adoption of the present
model hauling a train of standard Pullmans
near Flagstaff, Arizona.

THE DERNIER CRI IN 1887

The interior of the sleeping-car Santa Barbara,
built for the Espee in 1887 by Pullman, represented the last word in ornamentation and
what was then esteemed as "elegance." Its
seats upholstered in deep-red mohair; the
woodwork and trim were of mahogany, English oak and satinwood, all elaborately inlaid
and decorated with filigree and grille-work.
The illuminating lamps burned oil and coal
stoves were used for heating. Most Pullman
cars at this time, before the inauguration of
the dining-car on trains in the Far West, carried individual buffets for serving light meals
when trains did not stop at station restaurants.
Voyagers in an era of puff sleeves, Saratoga
trunks and Florida water rode in these wooden
museum pieces in the complacent knowledge
that the finest was none too good and that no
pains had been spared by the railroad to lap
them in tasteful and simple luxury.

Courtesy of the Southern Pacific

Maine—Maine Central Kennebec, and the Wabash's Banner Blue, and the long haul, transcontinental varnish of the order of the Santa Fe's Grand Canyon Limited, the Rock Island–Southern Pacific Golden State and the Chesapeake and Ohio's George Washington. The vast majority of these are standard fare trains and many of them have tourist-class accommodations, but in a few cases extra fares are required as the price of heightened speed and strictly *de luxe* equipment. The best-known extra-fare flyers are the New Haven's Merchants' Limited and Yankee Clipper, the Central's Twentieth Century, the Pennsylvania's Broadway, the Santa Fe's Chief and Super Chief, and the Chicago and North Western–Union Pacific–Southern Pacific Forty-niner.

Nor are all the handsome trains designed as the ultimate in passenger safety and comfort the great fifteen-car limiteds which figure so largely in the general imagination. Many are modest in their proportions and drawn by power that is far from modern yet maintained in the best style their lines can contrive. In this category of proud little varnish hauls fall such trains as the Monon's Tippecanoe, the Chicago and Eastern Illinois's St. Louis Zipper, the Boston and Maine's Pine Tree Limited, the Reading's Seven O'Klocker and the Nickel Plate's Nickel Plate Limited on the Chicago-Cleveland run. There is the Chicago and North Western's Minnesota 400, the Wabash's Banner Blue, the Western Pacific's Scenic Limited, the Seaboard Air Line's Florida Sunbeam and the Milwaukee's Tomahawk. There are coming into being, too, a number of up to the minute streamliners that embody all the artistry and technical perfection known to designers for comparatively short hauls such as the Boston and Maine's Flying Yankee, the New Haven's Comet, the Rock Island's Rockets, the Union Pacific's City of Salina and the Green Diamond of the Illinois Central. Luxury is becoming an integral part of the commuting traffic.

What is probably the last word, the phrase *fin de siècle* would be a most improper pun, in modern luxury is to be found in the private suite of the new streamlined Twentieth Century Limited, a *de luxe* apartment consisting of a spacious bedroom and drawing-room in harmonious shades of rust and pigskin gray with complete toilet facilities, located in the observation-car.

Ivan Dmitri

The Century, after 36 years of operation as the New York Central's crack limited on the New York–Chicago run, remains the outstanding flyer in the public imagination and, in fact, one of the fastest carded trains in the world, covering the 960 miles between its terminals, many of them through densely populated industrial sections abounding in railroad traffic, in a flat sixteen hours.

On its initial run in June, 1902, the Century was made up of four Pullmans and a restaurant-car of the currently standard design and made the run in twenty hours. The most recent version of the Century is composed of four super-trains of ten streamlined Hudson locomotives and

62 aluminum-alloy steel cars representing the designing genius of Henry Dreyfuss and an expenditure of several millions of dollars. The dignity of the train's tradition is emphasized by the simplicity of its decoration and color schemes, its luxury by rich materials and numerous new comforts and conveniences.

The exterior of the train is in two tones of gray from the sleek locomotive to the observation end. A dark gray band edged with blue runs the full length of the cars at the height of the windows and exposed rivet heads have been entirely eliminated. It is the first all-compartment train on any regularly scheduled run in America, all open berths having been supplanted by drawing-rooms, compartments and roomettes; and with the old familiar uppers and lowers disappeared, too, the strange jungle life which existed from time immemorial in the night-time aisles of the sleepers. Telephone systems connect the various cars, diners and clubs, costly flowers illustrate the interiors and at night, after passengers have retired, subdued blue lights illuminate the corridors and vestibules.

The luxurious resources of the Century make it virtually a smooth rolling hotel as it streaks across the Ohio and Indiana country-side. The observation-car features blue leather built-in couches, walnut writing-tables and book-racks and thick gray carpets. The side walls are of leather and at either end of the main lounge photomurals depict views of the terminal cities between which the train runs. A speedometer geared to the car trucks tells the passengers the rate of their acceleration.

There is a bar-lounge in rust and gray with brown cork walls and copper metal trim and an octagonal barber shop. The diner resembles the Colony Restaurant more than the familiar and traditional railroad restaurant-car. There are wall tables and arrangements for seating parties of from one to five, and at either end are intimate dining apartments with walnut walls, rust-colored ceilings and gray leather chairs divided from the principal restaurant by partitions of crystal clear, shatterproof plastic. During dinner a pre-arranged progam of classical music is played on a concealed phonograph.

Simultaneously with the placing in operation of the Central's new Twentieth Century Limited the Pennsylvania inaugurated four new streamlined luxury trains between the East and Middle West, the most celebrated of which was the line's Broadway Limited. All were designed by Raymond Loewy in collaboration with Pennsylvania engineers and, following the trend of modern train construction, emphasis was placed upon private bedrooms and compartments rather than upon old-style corridor sleeping accommodations. The new trains are the Broadway Limited and the General on the New York–Philadelphia–Chicago run, the Liberty Limited between Washington and Chicago, and the Spirit of St. Louis, the line's crack flyer between New York and St. Louis.

Perhaps the most remarkable of all recent railroad travel innovations has been the inaugural under the name El Capitan by the Santa Fe of a fleet of extra-fare all-coach passenger flyers duplicating the speed of the Super Chief and making the run between Chicago and Los Angeles in 39¾ hours. Designed along air-flow lines, light-weight and stainless, shot-welded steel, El Capitan is designed to provide competition for the Union Pacific famed Challengers and furnishes comfort and luxury on an economy basis for chair-car passengers. It is the first time, too, that an extra service charge has been levied aboard a train without sleeping or Pullman accommodations. Like the Santa Fe's new daylight trains, the Kansas Cityan, Chicagoan and San Diegan, El Capitan is Diesel-electric-powered and capable of high speed ranges. It has a capacity for 192 passengers and, like its opposition, Challenger, which covers the Chicago–Los Angeles run in two sections, one of coaches and one of tourist sleepers, El Capitan is one of the most heavily booked trains in the country, ranking in this category with the Southern Pacific's Daylight, the New York Central's Empire State Express and Commodore Vanderbilt.

Courtesy of the Southern Pacific

CAR HERALDS, DEVICES AND INSIGNIA OF THE PRINCIPAL RAILROADS OF NORTH AMERICA

CAR HERALDS, DEVICES AND INSIGNIA OF THE PRINCIPAL RAILROADS OF NORTH AMERICA

 Alton and Southern

 Apalachicola and Northern

 Arkansas Valley Interurban

 Atchison, Topeka and Santa Fe

 Atlanta, Birmingham and Coast

 Atlanta and West Point

 Atlantic Coast Line

 Baltimore and Ohio

 Bangor and Aroostook

 Belt Railway Company

 Bessemer and Lake Erie

 Canadian Pacific

 Canadian National

 Central of Georgia

Central of New Jersey

 Central Vermont

 Chicago, Attica and Southern

 Chicago, Burlington and Quincy

 Chicago and Eastern Illinois

 Chicago Great Western

 Chicago and Illinois Midland

 Chicago, Indianapolis and Louisville

Chicago, Milwaukee, St. Paul and Pacific

 Chicago, North Shore and Milwaukee

 Chicago and North Western

 Chicago, Rock Island and Pacific

 Chicago South Shore and South Bend

 Colorado Midland

 Colorado and Southern

 Delaware and Hudson

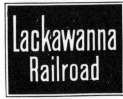 Delaware, Lackawanna and Western

 Denver and Rio Grande Western

 Dominion Atlantic

 Elgin, Joliet and Eastern

 Erie

 Escanaba and Lake Superior

 Fairport, Painesville and Eastern

 Florida East Coast

 Fort Dodge, Des Moines and Southern

Georgia

 Georgia and Florida

 Grand Trunk

 Great Northern

 Green Bay and Western

 Gulf, Mobile and Northern

 Illinois Central

 Illinois Central

 Illinois Terminal

 Indiana Harbor Belt

 Kansas City Southern

 Manitou and Pike's Peak

 Lackawanna and Wyoming Valley

 Minneapolis, St. Paul and Sault Ste. Marie

 Lehigh and Hudson River

 Minneapolis and St. Louis

 Lehigh Valley

 Missouri-Kansas-Texas

 Litchfield and Madison

 Missouri Pacific

 Long Island

 Mobile and Ohio

 Louisville and Nashville

 Nashville, Chattanooga and St. Louis

 Maine Central

 New York Central

 New York, Chicago and St. Louis

 Piedmont and Northern

 New York and Western Ontario

 Quanah, Acme and Pacific

 Newburgh and South Shore

 Quebec Central

 Norfolk and Western

 Reading Lines

 Northern Pacific

 Roscoe, Snyder and Pacific

 Pennsylvania

 Rutland

 Pere Marquette

 St. Louis–San Francisco

 St. Louis Southwestern

 San Pedro, Los Angeles and Salt Lake

 Seaboard Air

 Southern Pacific

 Spokane, Portland and Seattle

 Tennessee Central

 Texas and Pacific

 Toledo, Peoria and Western

 Union Pacific

 Wabash

 Western Pacific

A GLOSSARY OF RAILROAD TERMS, SLANG AND USAGE

A GLOSSARY OF RAILROAD TERMS, SLANG AND USAGE

AIR MONKEY: Air-brake repairman

ALLEY: Clear track in a switching yard

ANCHOR, TO: To set hand brakes on still cars

ARMSTRONG: Locomotive not equipped with a stoker

BATTLESHIP: Large locomotive

BEEHIVE: Yard office

BEND THE IRON: To change the position of a switch

BIG HOLE: Emergency position of the air-brake valve, causing a quick stop

BIG HOOK: Wrecking crane

BINDER: Hand brake

BLACK DIAMOND: Company coal

BLACK SNAKE: Solid train of coal-cars

BLAZER: A hot journal with packing afire

BLEED, TO: To drain air from a car or cars

BLEEDER: The valve by which air is bled

BOARD: Fixed signal regulating rail traffic, often referred to as slow board, order board, clear board or red (stop) board

BOILER WASH: A high-water engineer

BOOKKEEPER: Flagman

BOOMER: A drifting railroad worker, the opposite of a home guard. The term derives from pioneer days when railroads followed boom towns and camps.

BOUNCER, BED HOUSE: Caboose

BRAIN PLATE: Trainman's badge

BRAINS: Conductor

BRASS HAT: Rail official or executive

BRASS-POUNDER: Telegrapher

BREEZE: Service air

BROWNIE BOX: Superintendent's car

BROWNIES: Demerit marks, named after the originator of the system

BUG TORCH: Trainman's lantern

BUGGY TRACK: Caboose track

BULL: Railroad police officer

BULLNOSE: Front draw-bar of a locomotive

BUMP, TO: To secure another man's position through the exercise of seniority

BUMPER: Retaining post at the end of a spur track

CAGE: Caboose

CALLER: Employee, usually a boy, whose duty is to summon train and engine crews for duty

CAPTAIN: Freight or passenger conductor, a title dating from earliest railroading times when this was his official designation

CAR KNOCKER: Inspector

CAR TOAD: Car repairer

CHAIN-GANG: Train crew assigned to extra runs

CHARIOT: Caboose

CHASE THE RED, TO: To set out flag or red lantern to protect a train

CINDER CRUNCHER: Switch tender

CINDER SNAPPER: Passenger riding the platforms or observation seats where he collects cinders

CLUB WINDER: Brakeman

CLOWN WAGON: Caboose

CLUB: Three-foot hickory sticks used by freight trainmen to tighten hand brakes

COCK LOFT: Cupola of a caboose

COMPANY NOTCH: The notch on the reverse lever quadrant of a locomotive conducive to the most economical operation under given conditions

CONSIST: The make-up of a freight train in terms of car types

COON, TO: To go over the tops of the cars of a freight train

CORNER, TO: To strike a car which has not gone into the clear on a siding

CORN-FIELD MEET: Head-on collision between two trains using the same main track

CROW'S NEST: Cupola of a caboose

CRUMMY: Caboose

CUSHIONS: Passenger-coaches

CUT: A short string of cars coupled together or to a locomotive

DANCE THE CARPET, TO: To appear before an official for an investigation or for discipline

DEADHEAD: Employee or other passenger riding on a company pass; also empty passenger-car

DECK: Platform of the cab of a locomotive; also roof of a freight-car

DECORATE, TO: To go aloft to set the brakes of a freight train

DETAINER: Train dispatcher

DIAMOND: A crossover

DIAMOND CRACKER: Fireman

DIE GAME, TO: To stall on a hill

DINGER: Yardmaster or one of his assistants

DOG-CATCHER: Member of a crew set to relieve another which has been overtaken by sixteen-hour law

DOG-HOUSE: Caboose

DOLLY: Switch stand

DOLLY FLAPPER: Switch tender

DONIKER: Freight brakeman

DONKEY: Section man

DOPE: Official orders or instructions; company business; also composition for lubricating journals

DOUBLE, TO: To cut a train in half when encountering an insurmountable grade and carry it over in two sections

DOUBLE-HEADER: Train drawn by two locomotives

DRAG: Heavy train of dead freight; any sort of slow freight train

DRAW-BAR FLAGGING: Loafing on a brakeman's duties; to stay in the vicinity of a caboose when flagging instead of going back the distance required by regulation

DRILL CREW: Yard crew

DRONE CAGE: Private car

DROP: A switching movement in which cars are uncoupled from the locomotive and coast to their assigned places under their own momentum

DROPPER: A car rider in a gravity classification yard

DRUM: A hard-shelled conductor

DRUMMER: Yard conductor

DYNAMITER: A car whose defective air mechanism sends the brakes into full emergency when only a service application is made by the engineer

EAGLE-EYE: Locomotive engineer

END MAN: Parlor brakeman on freight train

ESPEE: The Southern Pacific Railroad

EYE: Signal

FIELD: Classification yard

FLAG: Brakeman sent out to protect the rear end of a train making an unscheduled stop; also an assumed name

FLAT WHEEL: A lame train employee

FLIMSY: Train order

FLYING SWITCH: Switching technique in which cars are cut off from behind a moving locomotive and the switch thrown after the engine has passed

FLY LIGHT, TO: To go on duty after missing a meal

FOG: Steam

FOOTBOARD: The step on the front and rear ends of yard or freight locomotives

FREEZE, TO: To cool an overheated journal

FROG: The X-shaped plate of a crossover; also an implement for re-railing car wheels

GALVANIZER: Car inspector

GANDY DANCER: Track laborer

GANGWAY: The rear portion of a locomotive deck

GARDEN: Freight yard

GATE: Switch

GENERAL: Yardmaster

GET THE ROCKING CHAIR, TO: To be retired on pension

GLORY: String of empties

GO HIGH, TO: To climb to the top of freight-cars for purposes of signaling or setting brakes

GON: A gondola-car

GOOSE, TO: To make an emergency stop

GRABBER: The conductor of a passenger train

GRAVEYARD: Spur tracks for obsolete or disused locomotives

GREASE MONK: Car oiler

GREENBACK: Frog for re-railing car or locomotive

GROUND-HOG: Brakeman

GRUNT: Locomotive driver

GUN: Torpedo used for signaling; also the injector of a locomotive

GUT: Air hose

HACK: Caboose

HAM: A student telegrapher or dispatcher

HARNESS: Dress uniform of a passenger conductor, blue tailcoat

HAY: Sleep on the job

HAY BURNER: Inspection torch

HEAD MAN: The freight train brakeman who rides the locomotive

HEEL: Car or cars at end of track with brakes set

HELPER: The auxiliary engine on a double-header

HERALD: The device, monogram or symbol of a railroad company, usually used as an identifying marker on freight-cars

HERDER: The mechanic who couples and uncouples locomotives at terminals

HIGHBALL: Signal for a clear track, deriving from the first train signals which were in the form of painted metal globes hoisted to the cross-arm of a tall pole when trains were to proceed

HIGHBALL ARTIST: Locomotive engineer noted for speedy running

HIGH DADDY: Flying switch

HIGH GRASS: Central New England Railroad

HIGH IRON: Main line or high-speed track

HIGHLINER: Main line express passenger train

HIGHTAIL, TO: To depart at a rapid speed

HIGHWHEELER: Old-fashioned type of passenger engine; also fast passenger train or limited

HIT THE DIRT, TO: To leap or fall off of a moving train, particularly when a wreck is impending

HOG: Locomotive

HOGGER, HOGHEAD: Locomotive engineer

Hog Law: The Federal statute providing that train or engine crews be removed from duty after sixteen hours of continuous service

Hole: Side track for passing trains on a single track line

Home Guard: An employee long associated with a single company, the opposite of boomer

Hook: Wrecking train

Hopper: Coal-car with hinged bottom for speedy dumping

Hoptoad: A derail iron

Horse over, to: To throw the mechanism of a locomotive into reverse position

Hot: With steam up

Hot box: Overheated journal or bearing usually resulting in burning journal packing

Hotshot: Fast train of any sort

Hump: Low knoll at end of classification yards down the slope of which freight-cars are allowed to glide to separate tracks by gravity

Humpback job: Assignment on a local way-freight train

Hut: Caboose

Indian Valley R.R.: A mythical road where there are always good jobs waiting; the happy haven of railway legend

In the ditch: Wrecked or derailed

Iron skull: Boiler-maker

Jack: Locomotive

Jam buster: Assistant yardmaster

Janney, to: To couple

Jay rod: Clinker hook

Jerk, to: To take up water for a locomotive from a track pan without stopping

Jerry: Section foreman

Jewel: Journal brass

Jigger: Full tonnage train of dead freight

Johnson bar: The hand-operated reverse lever of a locomotive

Juggler: Brakeman who must load and unload less than carload lots at way stations

Katy: The Missouri, Kansas, Texas Railroad

Keeley: Can of water to cool overheated journals

Kettle: Locomotive

Kick, to: To drop a car or cars

Kicker: Triple valve in defective order which throws air brakes into emergency when service application is intended

King: Yardmaster or freight conductor

King snipe: Foreman of a track gang

Ladder: Main track of a yard

Letter: Service certificate

Lightning slinger: Telegrapher

Liner: Passenger train

Link and pin: Old-fashioned or obsolete

Lizard scorcher: Train cook

Lung: Draw-bar

Main iron: Main track, high iron

Main pin: Executive

Manifest: Fast freight usually made up of merchandise, perishables or live stock

Marker: Rear-end signal of a train, flags or lights

Maul, to: To work an engine in corner with full throttle

Mill: Steam locomotive

Modoc: Employees' train

Monkey: Brakeman on cars in process of classification

Monkey house: Caboose

MOONLIGHT MECHANIC: Night round-house foreman

MOP: The Missouri Pacific Railroad

MOTION: The cross heads, side and main rods, eccentrics, link blocks, etc., the visible and moving driving-gear of a locomotive

MTYS: Empty freights

MUD CHICKEN: Surveyor

MUD SUCKER: A non-lifting injector

MUDSHOP: Yard clerk

MUZZLE LOADER: A hand-fired locomotive or obsolete type of power

NIGGERHEAD: Steam exit on top of locomotive boiler from which issue pipes to injector, etc.

NO-BILL: A non-union railroad worker

NOSE ON: Coupled to the front end of a locomotive

NUMBER GRABBER: Yard clerk

NUT BUSTER: Mechanic

NYPANO: The New York, Pennsylvania and Ohio Railroad, later part of the Erie

OP: Telegrapher

OPERATOR'S FIST: The distinctive, cursive type of handwriting characteristic of telegraph operators and train dispatchers

O.R.C.: Conductor, member of the Order of Railway Conductors

ORNAMENT: Station master

O.S., TO: To report a train by a station to the dispatcher

OUTLAWED: Suspended from duty by the terms of the sixteen-hour statute

PADDLE: Semaphore signal

PARLOR: Caboose

PARLOR BRAKEMAN: The one stationed at the rear end of a freight train

PECK: Twenty-minute stop allowed for a meal in a railroad restaurant

PEDDLE, TO: To set out freight-cars

PEDDLER: Local way-freight

PIG: Locomotive

PIG MAULER: Engineer

PIG-PEN: Roundhouse

PIKE: Railroad system

PIN, TO: To head for home; to pull the pin or knock off work

PIN PULLERS: Switchman who cuts off cars in train yard

PINK: Caution card

PINNER: Following switchman

PLUG: Throttle. In old days engineers were called plug pullers.

POP: Safety valve

POSSUM BELLY: Tool-box slung under a caboose

POUND HER, TO: To work a locomotive to capacity

PULL FREIGHT, TO: To depart or to give up a job

PULL THE PIN, TO: To knock off work or go home for the day

RABBIT: Derail iron

RAIL: Railroad man

RATTLER: Freight train

RAWHIDER: Executive or superior who is hard on his workmen

REAL ESTATE: Low grade coal

RED BALL: Fast freight train

RED UNION: Railroad eating-house

REEFER: Refrigerator-car

RINGMASTER: Yard master

RIP TRACK: Minor car repair siding

RIPRAP: Loose pieces of heavy stone or masonry used to protect from erosion road-beds exposed to water action

ROOF GARDEN: Helper locomotive on a mountain run

ROOFED: To be caught in close clearance

RUBBERNECK CAR: Observation-car

RULE G: Railroad regulation against drinking

SCOOP: Fireman's shovel

SENIORITY: The rights of passenger trains over freight and of express trains over locals; also the right of way in one direction on a single-track line

SHACK: Brakeman

SHANTY: Caboose

SHINER: Trainman's lantern

SHINING TIME: Starting time

SHORT: Car set out between stations

SHUFFLE THE DECK, TO: To switch cars on house tracks at every station

SHUNTING BOILER: Yard station

SIDE-DOOR PULLMAN: Box-car (hobo term)

SKIPPER: Conductor

SLAVE-DRIVER: A rawhiding executive or official

SLUG: Heavy fire in a locomotive firebox

SMOKE: Fireman

SMOKE ORDERS: Moving a train from one station to another without orders and by watching for the smoke of an approaching train on the same track; practiced in early years of railroading

SMOKER: Locomotive

SNAKE: Switchman

SNAKEHEAD: A rail coming loose from the ties and piercing a car floor; common accident among strap iron rails of a century ago

SNIPE: Track laborer

SNOOZER: Pullman car

SOFT BELLIES: Wooden frame cars

SPAR: Pole used to shove cars into clear when switching

SPEEDY: Call-boy

SPOT, TO: To place a car or engine in any designated position, specially in setting out freight-cars and making up freight trains

SPOTTER: A company inspector

STAB, TO: To delay or cause to lose time or precedence

STAR-GAZER: A brakeman who fails to observe signals

STEM WINDER: Climax-type geared engine

STICK: Staff used to control traffic on certain blocks of track and carried by engine crews to next station. The train carrying the staff has seniority.

STOPPER PULLER: Member of crew following engine in switching

STRAWBERRY PATCH: Rear end of caboose by night

STRING: Two or more cars coupled together; also telegraph wire

SUCK IT BY, TO: To make a flying switch

SWING: Brakeman in the middle of a freight train in charge of setting out cars and braking between the sections of the train handled by head and parlor brakemen

TAKE BY THE NECK, TO: When an engine pulls a drag up a steep grade

TALLOWPOT: Locomotive fireman

TANK: Locomotive tender

TEA-KETTLE: Any old or leaky locomotive

THOUSAND MILER: Dark blue shirt affected by railroad workers which doesn't show soiling over prolonged periods

TIE DOWN: To set hand brakes

TOAD: Derail iron

TOEPATH: Running board

TONK: Car repairer

TOP DRESSER DRAWER: Upper bunk in a caboose

TRAIN LINE: Main hose carrying compressed air to brake system

TRAVELING GRUNT: Road foreman of engines

TRAVELING MAN: Engineer of firemen unassigned to a regular run

TRICK: Shift, hours of duty

UNDERGROUND HOG: Chief engineer

VARNISH: Passenger-cars or train, dating from time when passenger equipment was highly lacquered

WABASH, TO: To corner a car

WALK AGAINST THE GUN, TO: To go up a stiff grade with the injector on

WALK THE DOG, TO: To wheel a freight so fast as to cause the cars to sway from side to side

WALSCHAERTS: The driving gear of a locomotive designed by Egide Walschaerts about 1900 in Belgium

WASHOUT: Violent stop signal made by waving both arms in a downward circle or by swinging lamp in wide, low semicircle across the track by night.

WAY CAR: Caboose

WHALE BELLY: Steel coal-car

WHEEL, TO: To drive a locomotive at high speed

WHISKERS: Age or seniority

WHISTLE PIG: Engineer

WHITE FEATHER: A plume of steam over safety valves indicating high boiler pressure

WILLIE: Way-bill for load-car

WIND: Air brakes

WING, TO: To set brakes on a moving train

WISDOM BOX: Yardmaster's office

WYE: "Y" tracks leading from a main line for turning around cars or engines where there is no turntable

YARD: System of tracks for the storage of cars or building trains

YARD GEESE: Switchmen

YARD GOAT: Switching engine

ZULU: Emigrant troup traveling by train

ZULU CAR: Emigrant car, particularly in Canadian railroading

BIBLIOGRAPHY

ADAMSON, ARCHIBALD, R.—*North Platte and Its Association* (North Platte, 1910)

Alta California Pacific Coast and Trans-continental Railroad Guide (San Francisco, 1871)

BAILEY, W. F.—*The Story of the First Trans-continental Railroad* (Pittsburgh, 1906)

BEADLE, J. H.—*The Undeveloped West; or, Five years in the Territories* (Philadelphia, Chicago, Cincinnati, St. Louis, 1873)

BELL, WILLIAM A.—*New Tracks in North America* (London, 1869), 2 Vols.

BOWLES, SAMUEL.—*Our New West* (Hartford, 1869)

CARRINGTON, COL. HENRY B.—*Ab-sa-ra-ka* (Philadelphia, 1878)

DODGE, MAJOR-GENERAL GRENVILLE M.—*How We Built the Union Pacific Railway* (New York, 1910)

DOLLFUS, CHARLES, and DE GEOFFROYS, EDGAR.—*Histoire de la Locomotion Terrestre* (Paris, 1935)

Files of the *New York Tribune*

Files of *Railroad Magazine*

Files of the *Sante Fe Employees' Magazine*

Files of *Scribner's Magazine*

FULTON, HERBERT WYNFORD.—*Epic of the Overland* (San Francisco, 1924)

HENRY, RALPH SELPH.—*Trains* (Indianapolis, 1934)

HUMASON, W. L.—*From the Atlantic Surf to the Golden Gate: First trip on the Great Pacific Railroad* (Hartford, 1869)

HUNGERFORD, EDWARD.—*Men and Iron* (New York, 1938)

MORFORD, HENRY.—*Morford's Scenery and Sensation Hand-book of the Pacific Railroads and California* (New York, 1878)

RAE, W. F.—*Westward by Rail* (London, 1871, 2d ed.)

RICHARDSON, ALBERT D.—*Beyond the Mississippi* (Hartford, 1867)

ROSS, JAMES, and GARY, GEORGE.—*From Wisconsin to California and Return* (Madison, Wisconsin, 1869)

SABIN, EDWIN L.—*Building the Union Pacific Railway* (Philadelphia, 1919)

STANLEY, SIR HENRY M.—*My Early Travels and Adventures in America and Asia* (New York, 1895) Vol. I

TRIGGS, J. H.—*History of Cheyenne and Northern Wyoming* (Omaha, 1876)

TROTTMAN, NELSON.—*History of the Union Pacific Railroad* (New York, 1923)